HOW TO SUCCEED AT WORK

HOW TO
Succeed at Work
Gaining the psychological edge

FRED E. ORR

UNWIN PAPERBACKS
Sydney London Boston

First published in Australia in 1987
by Unwin Paperbacks.
Second impression 1987

UNWIN PAPERBACKS
Allen & Unwin Australia Pty Ltd
8 Napier Street, North Sydney NSW, 2060 Australia

Allen & Unwin (New Zealand) Ltd
60 Cambridge Terrace, Wellington, New Zealand

UNWIN PAPERBACKS
18 Park Lane, Hemel Hempstead, Herts HP2 4TE England

Allen & Unwin Inc.
8 Winchester Place, Winchester, Mass 01890 USA

© Fred E. Orr 1987

National Library of Australia
Cataloguing-in-Publication entry:

Orr, Fred.
    How to succeed at work.

    Bibliography.
    ISBN 0 04 158009 5 (pbk.).

    1. Success in business.   I. Title.

650.1

Set in 10/11 pt Times by Graphicraft Typesetters Ltd,
Hong Kong.
Produced in Malaysia by SRM Production Services Sdn Bhd

Contents

Acknowledgements

Writing a book is in many ways a labour of love, but when the writing is substantially done in family time, the process can very easily create labouring love. Hence, I would like to thank my very understanding wife, Rachel, and my children, Matthew, Vanessa and Katharine, who tolerated my occasional absences, my silences and my infrequent moods. I would also like to thank Jill Hickson and Carol Serventy for their encouragement and their reading of the manuscript. Toby Marshall from Trans City Merchant Bank offered very helpful suggestions, as did Kerry Trembath and Sherene Suchy from the Careers and Employment Unit of the University of New South Wales. Finally, I would like to thank Patrick Gallagher and Roger Ward from Allen & Unwin for their readily available counsel and advice during all phases of the project.

Preface

This book is about work—or, more specifically, about the worker who wants to succeed at work by gaining the psychological edge. Essentially, succeeding at work involves becoming more effective and more efficient.

Work has been, and continues to be, a major concern for most individuals. Going to work satisfies at least two major needs— financial security and emotional fulfillment. This book is primarily about the latter: succeeding at work and gaining more satisfaction.

Underlying the following chapters are two assumptions: that most people want to perform well in their jobs; and that people can learn more effective work skills. The following chapters tell you how you can become a more efficient and more effective worker by developing and improving important skills such as time management, personal discipline and work concentration, to name but a few. Other chapters will discuss critical work-related skills such as how to: increase your confidence; boost your motivation; keep fit and beat stress; sharpen your communication skills; work more effectively with difficult people; manage love, hate and other strong emotions at work; make a case for promotion; explore new career possibilities; and leave your job constructively.

Why is it important for workers to learn how to improve their basic work skills? Firstly, because doing a better job is likely to make you feel better. Secondly, as the job market continues to become more competitive, you are more likely to prosper in your job if you are performing well. The worker who demonstrates increased personal effectiveness on the workfront will, it is hoped, win promotion and increased job satisfaction. Thirdly, unpaid workers such as housewives, and househusbands, and volunteer workers, will profit by knowing they are using their time and exercising their skills to the optimum.

Who will benefit from reading this book? Most workers, be they presently in jobs or unemployed but seeking work; employers;

personnel managers and trainers in industry; government employment officers; and finally, careers advisors, counsellors, and welfare officers—all will benefit from the messages contained in the book.

Various industries have recognised the need for in-house employee education and for years have sponsored a variety of education programs to assist and update their staff members. Some of the education programs have been technologically oriented, keeping the staff abreast of recent developments. Other programs have been focused upon the personal abilities of the workers, such as communication skills training. Private and public sector organisations have for years recognised the fact that workers are more productive and satisfied when they can work *and* learn.

As this book is about learning how to work more efficiently and effectively, it might be advisable to consider how you can use this book most appropriately. Some of the chapters will address issues of prime personal importance, while others could be of more marginal importance. Start with the chapters you identify as being immediately pertinent and put the principles into practice. Remember, working effectively and efficiently involves a set of skills which can be learned and improved, but practice will be necessary. The more you practice, the better your work effort becomes—and hopefully, the more positive the results you accrue.

At this point, I wish you happy reading, productive practising, prosperous working and ultimately, lots of success in your work.

1

Getting organised to succeed at work

'Some day I must get organised—but today I'm too busy!' We all know the feeling—dashing from place to place, sometimes forgetting important details, often backtracking to deal with overlooked matters. In more calm moments, you would probably agree that this is no way to run your life.

In many ways, succeeding at work is fundamentally a matter of getting organised. While you are calm, composed and considering various winning strategies, read on. This chapter will address the following practical and helpful ways of getting organised and becoming more efficient: using a daily plan; getting the important jobs done first each day; planning your tasks over longer periods of time; and giving some organised thought to your career.

To illustrate the need for an organised approach to your work, let's look at a brief case study of a disorganised person in distress. A friend, whom I shall call Charles, recently sought my advice because he was feeling extremely anxious and very depressed about going to work every workday. He teaches at a university, but his workdays have been devoid of satisfaction over the past year. He wakes up feeling restless and nervous and delays getting out of bed. His mind spins with a myriad of projects, lectures, meetings and other responsibilities which are awaiting attention. He openly admits that his work life is a shambles, but the trauma does not stop there. The guilt he feels about not being on top of his work responsibilities also affects his home life. His friendships are frayed and frazzled and his marriage fractured a few months ago.

What can be done to help the many individuals who present similar pictures of organisational chaos? For a start, it is important to admit to oneself that there is at least one significant problem impeding your daily effectiveness—a lack of organisation. While there could be additional problems requiring attention, you might want to start on the road to more productive and satisfying work experiences by assessing the location and depth of your organisational pitfalls.

Assessing your organisational pitfalls

Take a few minutes to read through the following list. Mark those items which relate to you.

( ) Much of my typical workday is wasted doing unimportant things.

( ) My work tends to get done in a 'helter-skelter' fashion.

( ) I often have difficulty sorting the important jobs from the trivial.

( ) I generally wait until the eleventh hour before getting down to work on major projects.

( ) I often start tasks but do not finish them.

( ) I am frequently indecisive about what to do next.

( ) I repeat work because of poor personal organisation.

( ) Friends and colleagues see me as being absent-minded or scatter-brained because I can't organise myself.

( ) I am not given jobs requiring greater responsibility.

( ) I have missed out on at least one promotional possibility because of being poorly organised.

Having read through the list and marked the items which characterise your work habits, you might find that the road to greater work productivity has many more pitfalls than you imagined. It might also be the case that some of the small holes in the road have much larger cavities beneath. Thus, your journey down the road to recovery will have to be strategically planned, starting with the first step—organising your days.

Organising your days, each day

Most people will say that they try to get their days organised in their minds, but they often forget things or find that they have to double back to do a task which should have been done earlier. Trying to remember all of the major jobs, not to mention the smaller tasks, can be a challenge. Do the people who carry major work responsibilities trust their memories? Generally, no. Most busy people write down their daily tasks: in a diary; on a desktop planner; or on a piece of paper which they carry in a pocket. Items on the list can be added to, deleted or changed as the day progresses.

While talking about organising your days, it is important to include non-work jobs which have to be done that day, perhaps on the way to or from work, or during one of your breaks. For example, if your mother's birthday is tomorrow, it is just not the same if she receives your birthday card the day following her birthday. Forgetting these personal duties can often create just as much trouble as missing a deadline at work. So, be certain to be thorough when constructing your list—include *all* work and personal tasks which require attention *today*.

Constructing your daily plan in the most efficient manner involves more than just listing jobs to be done. In order to remind yourself about the important jobs to be attacked first, rank them in order or use a highlighter to draw your attention to the top three jobs for the day. You might also want to specify the amount of time you believe will be necessary to complete the job. A 'done' column can provide some positive reinforcement when you tick the job on completion.

Let's look at a sample daily plan.

Daily plan

The Jobs	Priority	Time	Done
Pick up:			
Stationery			
on way to work			
122 High St.	1	5 mins	
Telephone:			
Bruce—Where Bronson file?	1	2 mins	
Kathleen—MAT meeting	1	5 mins	
Molly—lecture notes	1	15 mins	
Jack—conference plans	2	10 mins	
Theatre—Sat matinee	3	3 mins	
Letters/Reports:			
Start Smithson report	2	45 mins	
Write and post minutes			
of Plan'g Comm. Mtg.	1	90 mins	
Mrs Gray—thank you note	2	10 mins	

Daily plan

The Jobs	Priority	Time	Done
See:			
Robert re estimates			
for Ribley project	3	10 mins	
Sue—lunch	1	45 mins	
Buy:			
brown wrapping paper	3	5 mins	
Stamps, 10 aerogrammes	2	5 mins	
carrots)			
tomatoes)			
lettuce) way home	1	10 mins	
sausages)			
Exercise:			
walk to gym, workout	2	75 mins.	

The above plan has several features which will contribute to the effectiveness and efficiency of its user.

- Organise your jobs around the types of tasks to be done: picking up items, telephoning, letter and report writing, seeing various people, and buying necessary items. Depending upon the type of work you do, you may wish to organise the plan chronologically (morning, afternoon and evening sections) or perhaps even geographically by listing the various jobs according to your movements through the day. Try various types of plans and see which suits you best. The one essential ingredient is to write the jobs down. Very few individuals are endowed with fail proof memories—and on very busy days, chances are that your notes will be more reliable than your brain.

- Be precise in noting the tasks. For example, brief notes have been made after the names of the people to telephone. This might seem pedantic, but there is one very good reason for it. That is, most telephone calls take much longer than they need to. Ringing a colleague to confirm a meeting time or place might, under ordinary circumstances, take ten or fifteen minutes. However, if you have noted the specific reason for ringing Kathleen, you may be more likely to keep to the contracted task—getting to the point quickly and then getting off the phone. Making these task notes is particularly important if you really enjoy talking with Kathleen and vice versa. Time flies when positive emotions become involved. Enjoy the positive feelings, but also keep an eye on the clock and the remaining jobs on your daily plan.

- Give each job a priority rating: 1, 2, or 3. The success of the plan depends upon you getting started on the high priority jobs. However, some people have difficulty deciding which jobs are the most important. Preston, an engineer friend who teaches management skills, suggested the following solution to this dilemma:

  Construct two perpendicular lines, one for urgency and the other for importance. Label each line or axis with a high and a low. Then consider each job and plot its position. Those jobs which are plotted in the quadrant defined by high urgency and high importance should be labelled 1 on your plan. Those plotted in the quadrant defined by low urgency and importance should be priority 3 jobs. The others can be considered priority 2 jobs, unless there is a strong reason for labelling them otherwise. This is a sample chart:

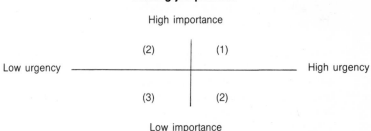

Plotting job priorities

High importance

| (2) | (1) |
Low urgency ————————————————————————— High urgency
| (3) | (2) |

Low importance

- Tick the 'Done' column to reinforce the positive feeling of accomplishment when you have completed a job. You might think this is somewhat elementary, giving yourself a tick upon job completion, but most people respond very positively to a pat on the back, even if it is self-administered. You can probably recall numerous occasions when you went out of your way to communicate subtly to your boss the fact that you had completed a difficult task. No harm in this whatsoever. Get all of the encouragement and praise you can wrangle from your boss and significant others, including yourself!

- When writing out your daily plan, do not schedule ten hours of high priority jobs for an eight hour working day. In fact, be certain to leave sufficient time for the unexpected—those URGENT jobs which have to done yesterday. The secret is to be determined and disciplined, but also flexible and adaptable. Daily plans which are ramrod rigid can crumble when crises occur. It's far better to bend with the new demands and weather the storm than to be blown over and flattened.

- Remember to include on your plan several tasks which can be done on the run, such as revising your part-time lecture notes while commuting on the bus or train. Newspaper and leisure reading can also be done while waiting for a scheduled appointment.

- Work weeks can sometimes extend into weekends. Without placing your home and possibly family life in jeopardy, try to accomodate unusual work demands by planning ahead and anticipating peak periods. If you must work on a weekend, plan your work precisely and be extra efficient so that you can get in and get out, preserving as much of your leisure time as possible.

- Planning your leisure might sound pedantic, but getting as much enjoyment as possible out of your recreational time is good commonsense. For example, planning the shopping trip to the gardening centre or the hi-fi store will save a double trip or forgotten-item frustration. You might want to forego the priority ratings and time limits on weekends, but list your leisure activities to get maximal value from your time.

- When planning your workdays, be certain to look ahead and give appropriate lead up time to planning and development activities for large projects looming in the distance. Read on for more about long-term planning.

Checklist to make daily planning work for you

You might say that you've tried all of this planning business before and it just doesn't work. Well, I can't offer an unconditional guarantee that planning your days will solve your organisational problems, but I can say that busy people generally do plan their work time and the planning makes them more time-efficient. The problem for the sceptics is probably more a case of putting the plan into operation. Chapter 3 addresses the issue of developing more self-discipline, but let's look at some ideas which might help you make this organisational plan operationally functional.

( ) Prepare a personal daily planning sheet and make some photocopies. Have your pad of planning sheets ready for use each day.

( ) Establish the habit of planning your day as soon as you get to work. Getting your tasks down in writing is the most important task at the start of your workday.

( ) Be sure that your planned projects and time limits are realistic. Trying to conquer too large a task in too short a time is only setting yourself up for failure—not a positively motivating experience!

( ) Reward yourself as you work through the tasks on your list, especially when you keep to the scheduled time.

( ) Build into your daily plans sufficient variety to keep you interested and motivated.

( ) Don't forget to add daily exercise to release any tensions generated at work or at home.

( ) Periodically assess your planning. Can it be done more effectively? Discuss your planning approach with a colleague respected for high efficiency.

( ) Practice saying 'No' to others who unnecessarily intrude. 'No' is a difficult word to say, but with conscientious practice, you should be able to say 'No' firmly, but with tact and diplomacy.

( ) Plan ahead for special leisure events and use these activities as rewards for getting specified high priority jobs done.

( ) Plan for some time each day for creative thinking, developing ideas or solving work-related problems.

( ) Feel good about becoming more organised. There's absolutely nothing wrong with becoming more time and task effective. Your boss will certainly agree!

Long-term organisational planning

Planning your days is the first step to becoming more organised and productive at work and at home. However, longer-term planning is also necessary to accomodate large projects and important events which require lead-up or preparation time. Taking time to plan your career goals is another long-term planning item which all too frequently is neglected. It is only when thoughts of leaving your present work preoccupy your mind that these longer-term plans are likely to receive ample consideration. Rather than put off your planning until these often chaotic and perhaps emotional periods, it's far better to give your career more frequent and rational consideration.

How can you make your planning for long-term projects and tasks at work more systematic and organised? There are several approaches you might want to try.

Firstly, enquire about yearly planners which are often available from stationery shops or from businesses using this medium to advertise their product or service. Your own employer might also have yearly planners available for employee use. These planners generally come as large printed sheets suitable for posting on a convenient wall near your desk or as desk top plastic mats. If you don't have the space to accomodate a large planning sheet, make your own smaller version on an index card similar to the one following.

Yearly planner

Jobs, events	Months											
	J	F	M	A	M	J	J	A	S	O	N	D
Jones Project			————————→M23									
AGM Papers			————————→Jn25									
Regional Trips		F4–M2								O1–N10		
Holidays						Jn27–Jl12						23→
Ames Project	→J3								→526			

Important dates:

	J	F	M	A	M	J	J	A	S	O	N	D
Anniv'y									A23			
R's B-Day											N14	
M's B-Day										O20		
V's B-Day					M19							
K's B-Day										O5		
School Hol's					M2–M17				A14–A22			
D14 ————————→F5												

There are several features of the Yearly Planner Chart which are worthy of comment.

- The chart should be easily seen so that you can be reminded daily about major projects and work tasks coming up in the future. Noticing that you have the Jones Project to submit on May 23 should prompt an early start. Large projects take considerable lead up time and you will probably be all too familiar with the discomforts of late night panic the evening before a major project is due.

- When plotting your committments, use lead-up arrows to indicate preparation time.

- Place your holidays on the chart so that you can take account of time away from work.

- Make notes on your planner about important birthdays and anniversaries. You might also want to note your children's school holidays, if relevant.

- Highlight various events using different colours of marking pens.

Thus, to make sure that you are working on schedule and remembering the important jobs and events looming in the future, use a visible and handy yearly planner. Take note of it daily to help you organise your tasks and your time.

Planning today for your career

Chapter 12 will deal in more depth with the topic leaving your job (and hopefully going on to better career prospects). At this stage, however, it is relevant to mention several career-related tasks which should be scheduled occasionally on your Daily Plan to enhance your career prospects.

1. Critically assess your present work skills.

In order to progress in your career, it will be necessary to assess your skills to uncover any deficiencies or weaknesses. As an aid, it might be helpful to read your job specifications which should be available from your boss. Alternatively, the required skills should be noted on your job advertisement, if you have retained the ad in your files. By the way, keeping your employment documents in a convenient file is always a good idea.

Check the skills which you should have mastered. If you have been in your job for a substantial period, you will probably be proficient in the skills which are used daily. However, it is common for job ads to specify skills which are less frequently used and therefore you may need to do some further training.

2. Participate in training and updating programs.

Most firms and large organisations will either have in-service training programs or will sponsor employees to enroll in external courses. For those working in large firms, your personnel office will be able to give you details about in-house programs and relevant external courses available locally or by correspondence.

3. Talk with senior people in your field.

Some very helpful advice can be obtained from people who have forged careers in your field. Take time to meet with these people and ask how they started and progressed.

4.   Get to know the people up the ladder in your organisation.

If you are interested in progressing in your organisation, it will be helpful to know the people who will be assessing your performance. This is not polishing the apple. On the contrary, it is *knowing* the apples—the good, the bad, and the indifferent. You can get to know these strategic people by participating on relevant committees, making worthwhile suggestions which will be considered at higher levels, and by becoming involved in your organisation's social activities, to name but a few possibilities.

5.   Schedule an appointment with your boss to discuss your career plans.

The most critical person who can influence your career in your organisation is your immediate boss. This person will be asked to write a report on your job strengths and weaknesses when you apply for promotion. So, before you reach that stage, discuss your current position and how you can enhance your skills and abilities.

Summary

Getting more organised is a skill which will make you more effective and efficient at work and more satisfied at home. This chapter has presented the following topics which will assist you to become more organised:

- Use a daily plan to list the jobs to be done, indicating their priority and a time estimate for completing the job
- Work to a daily plan each day
- Get to your high priority jobs first
- Reward yourself for completing each job
- Take time periodically to do long-term planning
- Use a yearly planner to schedule important projects and events
- Allow for ample lead-up time to get large jobs done
- Review your career plans regularly
- Assess your job skills
- Discuss your progress with friends, colleagues and your boss·

2
Managing your time efficiently

Getting on top of your time can be one of the most important aspects of working effectively and efficiently. You have to manage your duties at work, handle your responsibilities at home and arrange adequate leisure activities, to name just a few time-consuming activities. Making your time stretch across all of these functions can be a problem for most workers.

Regrettably, time can not be produced, stretched, stopped, nor turned back. The clock moves ahead with relentless regularity which can make it difficult to get your work done and enjoy your life. The major question is, how do you make time work for you?

This chapter will focus upon several themes: identifying time wasters; maximising your personal time at work, on the telephone, in meetings, with unwanted visitors, while commuting, when doing domestic duties at home, in front of the TV, and when waiting; and, using the important word, No, more frequently and effectively to save your time.

Perhaps the case of Marie might help to explain some of the points in this chapter. Marie is a single mother who works as an interior designer. While she is employed by a large firm, much of her work can be done at home. In addition to her paid work, she works very hard at managing three teenage girls, a domestic and family challenge for even the most effective person. Her time was under assault from many directions—shopping, cooking, cleaning (only when really necessary), pursuing her business, arranging for some relaxation and leisure time, not to mention trying to break into the telephone queue at home—a daily battle. Marie confronted her time problems and learned how to get more done in less time. You might find some of the suggestions which were discussed with Marie and which are presented in this chapter to be helpful as well.

Identifying time wasters

Looking back upon most days, you can generally discover without too much effort at least several periods of wasted time. 'But that's relaxation time' you might argue. Yes, some of this time might be used for rest and leisure, as long as they are not preventing you from getting on with your job. Apart from these quiet periods, how much other time during your days are you wasting? One way to answer this question is to keep a log of wasted time.

Buy a small notebook and jot down over the next two weeks the following notes about wasted time. No, these notes hopefully will not be a waste of time, but a valuable exercise in sensitising you to the subtleties of time maximisation.

Log of timewasters

Date ——/——/——
Timewasting event:
  When?
  Where?
  With whom?
  Why?
  Amount of time wasted:——————

Complete these notes each day for every timewasting event during the next two weeks. Try to be analytical and objective when evaluating your time usage. For example, ask yourself: Did that telephone call of twenty-five minutes really need to take twenty-five minutes?

At the end of the two week period, review your notes and look for any trends in time wastage. You might want to categorise your time wastage events into various classes, such as at work, at home, with colleagues, with family, waiting time, entertainment/leisure, etc. Having grouped your notes under the appropriate categories, add up the time wastage totals. If you have been fair and objective in appraising your time wastage, you will probably be quite surprised to find how large the figures are.

To double check your analysis, ask a person who knows you well for their opinion on how you use your time. You might ask them to comment, for example, upon the amount of time you spend speaking on the telephone, talking with other colleagues, attending meetings, dealing with correspondence, or saying No to unreasonable requests. Their view of you will be a valuable asset in helping you to become more efficient.

Having kept a time log over two weeks, Marie discovered that she spent an average of 67 minutes a day in what she termed wasted time—that's about five and half hours over a five day work week. Some of the major time wasters were: waiting for others to keep arranged appointments; waiting to get a chance to use the phone at home; commuting; and non-productive meetings at the office. We discussed how she could deal with these time wasters.

Time saving strategies at work

Saving time at the office or workplace is important for at least two reasons: 1, you can get more work done, thereby possibly earning you increased salary or promotion; and 2, getting more done makes you feel better about yourself—more competent, more confident. While some of your work duties will involve other people and thus may not be readily changeable, you can start with the aspects which are within your immediate domain, such as telephone calls and travel. Put the following pointers into practice to help you save time.

Telephone calls

Calls to others:
- Use the time while waiting for the other party to answer to plan what you are going to say.
- For very complicated calls, write out some brief notes as a rehearsal for the call. What are your reasons for making the call? How long should the call take?
- Use the telephone instead of writing a letter or memo—you can get the response immediately.
- Plan for a telephone call period daily and make calls in bulk.

Calls from others:
- Have all telephone calls screened, if possible. Be certain to thoroughly brief the person who will be taking your calls. Courtesy and thoughtfulness on their part can save you time and also goodwill.

- If you do not want to be disturbed, pull the plug on the phone.
- Do not hesitate to tell the other party that you are busy. Establish a mutually agreeable time to ring back.
- When all else fails and you are being bored by a garrulous caller, consider hanging up on the person *when you are speaking*. Then keep the receiver off the hook. If they ring back, they will think the telephone is out of order.

The telephone was a major source of bother for Marie. Her business depended upon clients and colleagues being able to reach her. During holiday periods when her daughters were home, they kept the telephone continually busy with prolonged conversations. The solution? Marie applied her interior design skills to the telephone problem and had an antique telephone booth with a pay phone installed in their spacious hallway. There was some initial expense in getting the equipment, but the time saved quickly paid for it. Of course, the girls had to pay for their own phone calls, which helped to curb their telephone behaviour.

Commuting and work-related travel

Those workers who live in cities and commute to work by car, might find some of the following suggestions to be time savers.

Why not start by questioning the basic necessity of having your car sitting in a parking space during your work hours. Is public transport an option? Aside from the considerable financial saving in purchase and maintenance costs, you can use your commuting time more effectively by taking public transport. Commuting time can then be used for work preparation, recreational reading, planning, or just relaxing. If your job requires you to have a car in steady use or at least at call, some of the following pointers may be applicable.

Time savers for commuters

- Use a tape recorder to prepare notes while travelling or to listen to educational tapes.
- Upgrade your qualifications by doing a taped correspondence course while commuting. Carry a portable tape playback machine with you with an ear plug attachment so that you can also listen in public places.

- You can practice relaxation exercises at red traffic lights by using your hand brake and then letting your body relax in the driver's seat.

- Bicycling or walking, if circumstances allow, can be convenient ways to combine travelling to work and getting routine daily exercise.

- If driving your car to work is a must, listen to the radio traffic reports so to avoid congested areas.

- A pre-paid parking space can save you hassles and time, and your time is probably more valuable than the parking fees.

Marie was studying Italian as an evening student and prepared revision tapes for use in her car. For example, she would record each new word or phrase, followed by a brief pause, and then the English translation. She was thus able to revise the vocabulary *in transit* and save valuable desk time for more demanding study tasks.

Meetings

Meetings at work can occupy many frustrating hours. Even though they are very time-expensive (given the total of the hourly salaries of all participants), they are often considered to be organisational rituals held as a habit, often with nothing of consequence to discuss. In addition to being regular rituals, meetings can also be the posturing place for upwardly mobile office politicians. No matter what the motives might be for holding office meetings, be carefully critical about whether the meetings will be wasting *your* time.

- Suggest to the group which is holding a meeting that an agenda be circulated prior to the meeting and that it be followed during the meeting.

- If you are very busy, convey your apologies to the chair for not attending.

- Suggest that meetings be cancelled if there is no important business to be discussed.

- Use memoranda instead of meetings to circulate information.

- Try holding your meetings in a room without any seats to

save time. Standing meetings generally take less time than sitting meetings.

Marie and her colleagues developed an agenda format which reserved the right side of the paper for thoughts, comments, objections and other important notes. If the individual was not able to attend, their notes could be considered in their absence. Encouraging colleagues to think through the issues on the agenda beforehand also expedited the progress of the meetings.

Office visitors

Just when you want to get some important job done and you've made a start, it's uncanny how the office gossip or another equally garrulous person invades your workspace. It can seem that these people monitor your mind and gear their visits to guarantee minimal work output from you. How can you deal with these unwanted visitors without being rude? Try these suggestions for a start:

- If you have an office door, keep it closed when you do not want to be disturbed.
- If possible, try to arrange for someone to intercept visitors and take messages for you.
- Go to others before they come to you. It is far easier to terminate conversations when you are at the other person's workplace. Saying, 'I've got to go now.' will usually suffice.
- If you hear the office talker coming down the hall, jump up from your desk and place yourself diagonally across your office door jamb. Whatever you do, do not allow the person to enter your workspace.
- As noted above, standing discussions take far less time than sitting discussions. If the office talker does gain entry to your office and, Heaven forbid, gets seated, do not sit down yourself. Stay standing and make unwelcoming gestures like looking at your watch or pacing in ever decreasing circles around the intruder's chair. The intruder will soon leave.
- Practice terminating phrases, such as: Well, then, it seems that ... or, In essence, it can be concluded that ... to give notice to the other party that you want to draw the conversation to a close.
- Observe the nonverbal signals of good time managers, such

as closing desk top files or uncrossing legs and moving to the front of the chair. Body language alone can effectively communicate the end of a discussion.

- List matters which require only short discussions with others and discuss them during coffee breaks or over lunch.

Domestic engineering

Saving time around the house is equally important as saving time at a place of paid employment. The pressures are often just as high and the responsibilities are frequently more diverse. Try the following suggestions to increase your efficiency at home.

Shopping, outings and household delegating:

- Keep a family diary by the telephone for recording all commitments and essential information (e.g., school holidays, evenings out, dinner guests, overnight visitors, and other special events).
- Find a handy spot in the kitchen for recording shopping items and record them as you run out.
- When planning your shopping trip, organise your list according to the layout of the goods in the shop.
- Delegate the shopping to the older children (if present) and reward them for work well done.
- Delegate dish washing and other household chores to older children. Use a roster system if convenient.

Marie followed a domestic policy of tough love in order to get all of the domestic chores accomplished. She asked her daughters to devise a rotating roster which included all of the normal household chores plus car and garden maintenance jobs. She believed that teaching the girls to accept responsibility for their living conditions was important. It also made her job as mother and domestic engineer easier.

The family car:

- Place a keyboard near your most used exit door for hanging car keys. Place a spare set in a safe place elsewhere in the home and perhaps one in a magnetised case under a mud guard or behind the license plate for when your regular set goes missing. (It happens to everyone!)

- For child pickup and delivery, try to organise a car pool so that others share the driving time.

Household time savers:

- Place a small table or shelf near your most used exit door for depositing things which must be taken elsewhere (library books for return, dry cleaning, films for developing, etc.).
- Place another small table near the bottom of your stairs for depositing items which must be taken upstairs.
- Arrange a convenient hanging line in the laundry so that drip dry articles can be hung up as soon as they are taken from the washing machine or dryer.
- Place a storage cupboard next to the water heater or dryer for keeping items which must be maintained in dry conditions.
- Carry a handy basket with you as you tidy the house so that misplaced items can be collected in one trip. Encourage family members to be responsible for their own possessions.
- In order to salve your conscience about very sloppy and disorganised children's bedrooms, place a sign on each bedroom door: The orderliness of this bedroom is the sole responsibility of *(name of child)*.
- Cook in large quantities and freeze one-person portions for the occasional late meal.
- In order to ease the morning rush, make children responsible for their own time. If they dawdle before school, let them be late and suffer the consequences. They will learn if they are made responsible for their own behaviour.

For most people, television offers an appealing allure. You can argue very strongly that watching it will relax you or less strongly that it will keep you informed and up-to-date. The harsh truth is that most television is designed as pure entertainment—even the news! There's nothing wrong with entertainment, except for the fact that it is quite easy to spend too much time in front of the television set and ignore other jobs. Waging a time battle with the TV set can be a test of personal discipline.

Managing television time

- Read the program guide and mark interesting shows with a highlighting pen.
- Realise that turning on the television set takes very little personal energy, but turning it off can pose a considerable challenge.
- Try standing when you want to watch only the news or other short programs. (It's easier to move away from the set when the program ends.)
- For longer shows, set the oven timer or a wrist alarm to go off at the end of the program. Move away from the set when the alarm sounds.
- For the ultra-weak who find the TV set too alluring, place the set in a very unappealing place, such as in a storage room with no seats or in a musty basement. Make TV watching difficult or even aversive.
- The definitive solutions for TV addicts—sell the set, give it away or even place your boot through the tube. (Turn the set off first!)

Utilising your waiting time

Waiting time can be frustrating and annoying, but it seems to be part of most people's daily life. The waiting periods might include waiting to be served in a shop, waiting in waiting rooms (to see a doctor, dentist, etc.), waiting for the other party to answer the phone, waiting for a friend at lunch time, waiting in a traffic jam, to name but a few possible waiting situations. Try the following suggestions to make your waiting time more productive and beneficial.

Waiting while shopping:

- As a general rule, try to avoid waits by shopping and travelling outside of peak hours.
- If shopping during a busy period, be certain to position yourself strategically at shop counters so the shop assistant is in no doubt about whom to serve next.

- Be quite prepared to say to queue jumpers: Excuse me. I am next to be served!
- When shopping for specific items, do it by telephone and have the purchases delivered, if possible.
- Consider shopping from mail order catalogues. No traffic, no parking and no shop counter waiting.

Waiting on the telephone:

- When placing calls to parties who have very busy periods, call at off peak times.
- Organise your telephone table or desk so that you can write or read while waiting on the telephone.
- If a switchboard operator puts you through to an extension but there is no answer, jiggle the hangup button in order to get back to the operator to leave a message.
- If calling long distance, be certain to say to the answering party: I am calling long distance for ....—so that waiting will be minimised.

Waiting in waiting rooms:

- If you have a doctor's appointment and from past experience have found the waiting room to be full on your arrival, telephone ahead and ask what delay is anticipated.
- Make appointments for the first time slot in the consultation period so that you are not faced with the all too common, 'The doctor is running a bit behind schedule'.
- Always take your own reading material, as waiting room magazines can be dated or of no personal appeal.
- If you have generally been kept waiting for more than 30 minutes over several different appointments, tell the person with whom you have the appointment that you would appreciate every effort in keeping to the scheduled appointment time, as your time is important too.

Waiting in traffic or public places:

- When in a traffic jam, relax your white-knuckled grip on the steering wheel and practise relaxation exercises. (See Chapter 7 for details.)
- If you are planning to venture into the depths of a traffic-

congested city, consider parking at a suburban train station and taking a train to avoid the waiting.

- Brush up on your music appreciation via tape or radio while you are waiting in traffic.
- Consider the possibility of installing a mobile telephone so that you can catch up on your calls while waiting in traffic.
- Enquire about flexitime working hours so that you are not travelling during the peak commuting times.
- If caught without a book or other resources, study the people around you, any observable wildlife or even the weather patterns. An absorbed mind will make the waiting time pass more quickly.

Marie found an assertiveness training class did wonders for her time management. Shop assistants always noticed she was next to be served because of her upraised hand and index finger. Her doctor learned to respect her appointment time after being tactfully reminded that time was important to her as well. By circulating a car pool questionnaire to the relevant families involved in similar activities, she arranged a shared transport system of value to all concerned. Marie solved many time problems with some creative thinking and forthright behaviour.

Summary

Managing time well is the hallmark of an efficient worker. Most people can name several busy people who always seem to be on top of their time. They are well-organised, prepared for the hassles of everyday life and they are self-disciplined. This chapter has presented some time management strategies which might help you to become more time effective:

- More efficient use of telephone talking time
- Less interruptions by incoming telephone calls
- Saving time in meetings
- Preventing unwanted office visitors from distracting you
- Using your commuting time more effectively
- Organising your house and your housemates to help save your time
- Dealing with domestic driving tasks most efficiently
- Using waiting time in shops, on the telephone, in waiting rooms, and in traffic jams to best advantage

By implementing the suggestions described in this chapter, you should find that you will not only get more work done, but you will also generate self respect. Being on top of your time generally means that you are in more effective control of your life—and that is a very pleasant and productive state of being.

3

Developing self-discipline

How often ...

- Have you been incapacitated by indecisiveness?
- Have you spent valuable time writing out detailed plans but left them untouched and unheeded?
- Have you avoided doing the really important job and substituted instead several easily achieved but trivial tasks?
- Have you felt incompetent and incapable because you failed to meet yet another deadline?
- Have you lost promotion opportunities because others were found to be more reliable?

The list of how oftens could go on and on, mainly because the items centre upon one of the most common weaknesses of workers: lack of self-discipline. Self-discipline is very important in succeeding at work. It enables you to gain satisfaction and hopefully win justified praise and possibly promotion. Apart from progressing in your work, becoming more self-disciplined can also enhance your personal and domestic life. In essence, self-discipline is an important attribute which can advance many aspects of your life. At work, self-discipline means that you get going quickly, work effectively and finish reliably.

Becoming more self-disciplined is a goal sought by most workers. However, it is frequently an elusive quality. Why? Chiefly because it means the worker may have to learn some new and potentially difficult behaviours, like beating procrastination. Becoming more self-disciplined might also involve learning how to be less of a perfectionist (I won't start until I can do it perfectly) or learning how to overcome a strong fear of failure. These are all lessons requiring hard work.

This chapter covers 'becoming more self-disciplined' and 'overcoming procrastination'. Before accusations can be levelled at me about putting off starting these difficult topics, let's get straight to work.

Becoming more self-disciplined

Bruce, an architect whom I have known for many years, excels at his work—but, only when he can work up the courage to put his ideas down on paper. He works from home and always finds small domestic jobs which, he argues, require his immediate attention. These urgent household jobs seem to pop up almost daily, causing him to be absent from his workroom. Even after settling at his drawing desk, he complains of wandering thoughts and inability to get started. He says that the size and complexity of his projects often intimidate him. While his work is well-regarded, Bruce rarely meets deadlines—creating difficulties for himself and his clients. After losing several large contracts, he sought my advice about how to become more reliable at work.

Bruce's dilemma is quite common. Part of the problem lies in the nature of his particular work—its subjectivity. What is an appealing design to one person can be appalling to another. Although most workers are not in the creative arts, the suggestions I made to Bruce are generally applicable to them.

This section will present five steps which you can use to become more self-disciplined: getting settled at your workplace; defining the jobs to be done; dividing the large jobs into manageable tasks; establishing realistic deadlines; and setting specific rewards for achieving your work goals.

Step 1   Get settled at your workspace!

Getting down to work can be a surprisingly difficult task, especially if the job to be done threatens you in some way. Perhaps the job will tax your limits or pose a new and difficult problem which must be solved? In response to these work threats, most of us have sought relief in tasks like sharpening the next half-dozen pencils.

When there is a job to be done, get your materials together and attack the task straight away. Be very aware of devious internal voices suggesting enticing work alternatives. Be firm—get to the task!

Under some circumstances, starting a work task can make you

feel highly nervous and anxious. If you are feeling restless before you start the job, try the following exercise:

> Sit comfortably at your workplace, close your eyes and take a comfortably deep breath. As you breathe out, allow your shoulders to drop, feeling as much tension as possible draining away from your body. Try it right now. Feels good to let the tension go, doesn't it? Use this exercise whenever you feel tension building up at your workplace. It will help you to feel more relaxed and able to get down to work.

Another way to form the habit of reliable work is to use an external signal or stimulus to prompt productive work behaviour. For example, when I was at university, I often had difficulty getting settled for evening study. I tried changing from my daytime clothes into jeans and a comfortable tee-shirt. Over a few weeks, these clothes became my study uniform. Getting changed into these clothes helped establish the mental attitude that I was ready for work. You might not be able to don a tee-shirt, but you might be able to put on a special watch or some other small item to create a go signal. If you enjoy a more antiquated approach, why not make yourself a pair of elastic arm bands like those used in yesteryear to hold up long shirt sleeves. Those bands were commonly used in offices by workers as alternatives to a rolling the sleeves up approach to their work. No matter what system you choose, condition yourself to respond immediately, positively and productively to getting started on your work.

Once you are ready for work, stay put. If your mind keeps thinking of other important matters, write the items on a list and deal with them later. The important points are to GET TO YOUR WORKSPACE, GET SETTLED AND THEN GET STARTED.

Step 2 Define the task(s)

Having established yourself at your workspace, the next step is to define specifically what is to be done in that work period. Do not approach your work with the aim, I'll now do a bit of work. Using a goal such as this is far too general and leaves you potentially open to distraction. For example, if you receive a call from a colleague inviting you to go elsewhere for a discussion, you could possibly say to yourself, 'Yes. I've done a bit of work, so I'll go up and see Steve.' It's far better to be task and time specific. That is, write your specific goal onto paper and estimate the time needed to finish that task.

Another advantage of writing down a work contract with yourself is that you can feel justifiably satisfied when you have completed the task. For example, imagine the frustration of running in a race but not knowing where the finish line is. Being uncertain abut completing the race robs you of that positive feeling of accomplishment as you cross the finish line. The same rewarding feeling is perfectly appropriate to your work setting. Specify the end point of your tasks for each work period so that you can feel justifiably satisfied at job completion.

Step 3   Divide large jobs into manageable tasks

Imagine yourself as a worker looking skyward at a mountainous pile of work which must be accomplished. Standing in the shadow of such a mountain can be frightening, perhaps even paralysing. You might be thinking, My God. How will I ever get this mountain moved?

Assuming that your boss expects you to conquer this mountainous job and the request is reasonable, then the task should be achievable. So it's just a matter of organising your approach. Where should I start? is the usual question of workers contemplating a large and perhaps complicated job. Think about the job and try to see it from a different perspective. Just as most mountains are composed of smaller units, usually rocks and boulders, see if you can divide your jobs into more manageable tasks and then get to work on the first part.

I vividly recall my first interview with my doctoral thesis supervisor. He pulled out a copy of his Ph.D. thesis, a volume about four inches thick, and said, 'This is the type of challenge confronting you over the next few years.' My knees suddenly became weak and jelly-like. I previously had written major reports but nothing of the size he was suggesting. Being an astute psychologist, he noted my obvious distress and suggested I sit down before collapsing. He then explained that his thesis was composed of twelve chapters and each chapter contained about four to six sections. Each section contained several subsections and any one of these might be composed of, say, ten to twenty paragraphs. He asked if I could write a paragraph to which I heartily said, Yes. He responded, 'Well, then, you're on your way.

Once you have determined the thesis' structure, it's just a matter of working from one paragraph to the next, making certain that each leads logically on to the next.' At the end of the interview, I did feel more reassured, even though the task still looked absolutely gigantic.

By starting with small and manageable tasks such as writing a paragraph, you have the distinct advantage of feeling early in the job that you are making progress. The progress might be small and apparently insignificant at first, but the important point is that you have started and are moving ahead. You have overcome the first obstacle—getting started. Your early momentum should be a considerable advantage as you take on succeeding challenges. The important point is to keep the momentum going!

Step 4   Establish realistic deadlines

This step is essentially self-explanatory as most people try to use deadlines to prompt improved work performance. However, many workers have established job deadlines which have been patently unrealistic. Expecting yourself to do ten hours work in four or five hours is just setting yourself up to fail. And, to fail time after time is discouraging. It's better to set no deadline than to court inevitable failure.

Depending upon the type of work you do, you may want to establish your deadlines by the hour, by the day, or by the week. If you use longer time periods than one week, you may lose some of the motivating qualities of feeling that progress is being made. As suggested above, look at your work and break the task down into parts. Then set a realistic time limit for completion of the various parts. Once you have established a reliable deadline system, you should be able to reap a bountiful harvest of self-satisfaction from accomplished work.

Step 5   Set rewards for work accomplished

Developing greater powers of self-discipline can be hard work, requiring at times some psychological pain in order to reverse old and comfortable habits of delay and avoidance. Taking on an intimidating job or trying your hand at a new skill can be threatening, so you will want all of the encouragement you can muster.

The encouragement can be various rewards which you set for

yourself. What sort of rewards should you use? Think about the things which give you a lot of pleasure. Make a list of them for variety's sake. Seeing a movie, taking a walk, eating an apple or contacting an old friend are some reward suggestions. Ensure that the rewards are appealing and worthy of the effort. They should also be scheduled frequently, say every two hours or so to maximise your work effort.

In summary, developing more self-discipline will require hard work and perseverance, but the end result will be very worthwhile. You will need to be rigorous with yourself. Establish an effective routine of getting settled, defining the tasks to be done, breaking the big jobs down into manageable tasks and using enticing rewards to prompt ongoing action.

Overcoming procrastination

Procrastination can be a deeply entrenched behaviour pattern which, unfortunately, can decidedly wreck your work life. Putting off a job until later is comfortable, but that is generally not what your boss wants. What can you expect if you are consistently unreliable? Promotion? Hardly. Performing well at the workfront generally means being punctual, dependable and reliable. These are very nice characteristics to have, but for the procrastinators, they are challenging behaviours to acquire.

So what can be done to get on top of procrastination and become more reliable? To begin with, you will have to act firmly. Comfortable habits such as procrastination are notoriously difficult to budge. If you are a habitual procrastinator, try the following suggestions.

Post a sign on your bathroom or bedroom mirror: I will not procrastinate today! As you prepare for the day, recite the saying several times. Starting each work day in this way will sensitise you to the problem behaviour.

Having begun your working day on a firm and positive bearing, sit down and organise your daily plan as soon as you arrive at work. As a procrastination-prone person (and who isn't), be certain to ask yourself, What are the MOST IMPORTANT jobs for me to get going on today? Having listed the jobs, check if there are any crucial jobs which you have temporarily shelved because they are too difficult, or because you just aren't in the mood for them today. These shelf jobs are probably the ones which create anxiety and tension. If you discover one or two jobs on the too difficult shelf and they are important, get them down and straight onto your daily plan. Confront any temptation to procrastinate, especially during the important planning stage of the day.

What if these suggestions don't work?, you might ask. If you have tried the five steps on several different occasions and the result is no better than before, then perhaps one of the following situations prevails:

- You are experiencing an unusually high fear of failure which impedes you from taking even the slightest risk.
- You are a perfectionist and believe that the task is not worth starting if you can not do a 100 per cent job.
- You are severely affected by the comments and possible criticisms of others and defer from trying new or challenging tasks.

Let's look at each of these procrastination situations in more detail.

Conquering fears of failure

Fear of failure is surprisingly common. Recall your last job or promotion interview. Your pulse rate was probably higher than normal and your mind was most likely racing—trying to rehearse how to respond to the difficult questions which you were anticipating. If your work is adversely affected by a pronounced fear of failure, then confront the problem and deal with it objectively. After all, the worst possible outcome of trying a work task and then failing is probably transient embarrassment. You might be embarrassed for a while, but that will fade. The residue hopefully will be a valuable learning experience. Trial and error learning is a time-honoured process and one familiar to most successful workers.

If your anxiety level is high when approaching certain aspects of your work, be certain to read and apply the relaxation techniques described in Chapter 7. You are far better off replacing anxiety feelings (heart palpitations, rapid and shallow breathing, sweaty palms, shaky limbs, to name a few symptoms) with cool, calm composure. Learning to relax takes time and practice, but the results will be very worthwhile.

Once you have established a reliable relaxation response, you can use a process called systematic desensitisation to remove unrealistic fears. This is how it works. Write out a list of anxiety provoking tasks which have caused you to procrastinate in the past. Having listed them, organise the list in ascending order, that is from the least to the most threatening tasks. With your list at hand, stretch out for a relaxation session and when fully relaxed, read your first item and visualise yourself in the first situation. Make the situation as real as possible by focusing upon the sights, sounds, textures, smells and, if relevant, the tastes which might apply to the particular situation. You want to be able to step into the scene and be part of it.

Here's a sample item from a desensitisation hierarchy to illustrate the amount of detail which is desired:

Item 8 (fairly far up on the list—a difficult item)

Today is the day when I have to meet with the departmental heads to present my final progress report. The committee will expect me to specify the completion date. I'm sitting at my office desk 20 minutes before the meeting starts. I have all of the project papers stacked in front of me. I can feel the chair upholstery and I shift my weight in my seat. The typing noises in the background sound louder than normal. I catch the occasional whiff of coffee aroma from the coffee machine down the hall. I can see the second hand of the wall clock moving relentlessly around the dial as the minutes fly by.

While not trying to be overly dramatic, the scene is meant to be sufficiently realistic to allow you to strongly identify with it and hopefully become part of it. Note that the sights, smells, sounds and textures all help to make the scene immediately real. Try to use similar physical descriptors when writing out your own items.

If, while visualising any scene, you experience some anxiety feelings, then say Stop! to yourself and picture in your mind a STOP sign. Having interrupted the anxiety response, then say Relax to yourself to restore a feeling of calmness. When fully relaxed again, repeat the scene and try to hold the image for about fifteen seconds. When you are able to hold an image of yourself performing in an effective and productive way in the present scene, then progress to the next item. If practical, try to organise a similar situation at your workplace. By using this step-wise approach, you will be able to overcome much of the anxiety which has hampered or hindered your previous work efforts.

Becoming less of a perfectionist

Being a perfectionist is laudable in some work areas such as brain surgery and aircraft maintenance, but in most other types of work you are putting yourself at a serious disadvantage if you demand a perfect outcome in every attempt. Expecting perfection is demanding and generally frustrating for most workers—especially when they fall short of the mark. The more important goal is a willingness to try and not be put off by failure.

The importance of trying is implicit in the adage often quoted by business management experts: *Those who are not trying and many times failing are either stagnant or dead.*

The significance of this saying is that progress generally occurs when people try. Let's say that you have been working in your job for several months and have been reluctant to try some new ideas because they might not be perfect. In the past, you may have argued to yourself that it is better to be entirely safe and certain before committing yourself to anything new. However, you may have found that holding back is really getting you nowhere, except into a more deeply entrenched and stagnated position.

How can you break down procrastination based upon a quest for perfection? Here are a few suggestions which might help:

- Study the strengths and weaknesses of other workers around you. Assuming you are working with real people and not fail-proof robots, you will quickly find that we are all composed of strengths and weaknesses. That is the human condition, like it or not. Seeing the weaknesses of those around you may help you to accept your own.

- Read biographies. If the biographer has presented a true and balanced picture of the subject's life, you should be able to identify strengths and weaknesses. The very fact that the person's life is the basis of a published biography suggests a significant contribution was made—in spite of personal weaknesses.

- Talk about your strengths (with tact) and your weaknesses with your friends. Discussing your inadequacies can be helpful, especially if your friends are understanding and supportive.

- Practice taking calculated risks outside the workplace. Choose an activity in which your confidence is high, such as a hobby or sport. For example, if you are a golfer, suggest pairing up with a slightly better player rather than sticking with your regular partner. Be prepared to try, lose and then try again. It's the spirit of the activity and not the final result which is important.

- Tell a close friend about your campaign of courage. Suggest that you meet weekly to discuss the risks you have taken over the past week and to set specific targets for the following week. You'll find yourself working much more conscientiously on your campaign if you have to account to a friend at the end of a week about your efforts and your results.

Working in spite of unjust criticism

Constructive criticism can be very helpful in shaping more effective work performance and you should welcome every opportunity to receive this valuable commentary. However, not all criticism is constructive and well-intentioned. Most of us can vividly recall receiving blatantly unjust, unfair and perhaps even malicious criticism in the past. These destructive remarks hurt. Many people are put off risk taking if they face a vitriolic backlash from their boss or colleagues. We learn to avoid doing things which cause hurt, especially emotional hurts.

How can you deal with a fear of criticism? One approach is to examine the criticiser. Ask yourself if the person is trying to demean you. Are my actions in some way threatening this individual? Is the criticiser boosting his or her own wilting ego by demeaning me? Asking these questions might help you to understand the situation and thus be less traumatised by the criticisms.

Take note that criticism is often a disguised compliment.

Throughout history, it has typically been the doers of society who have been the subject of frequent and often quite abusive criticism. See yourself as a doer, a person who has had the courage to get out and try, hopefully to succeed, but certainly to learn. Your experiences will boost your confidence and encourage you to keep going. Thus, see criticisms as objectively as possible. Learn from them and do not be deterred if the remarks seem unjust and unfair. Press ahead with courage and conviction.

There is one more aspect about unjust criticisms which you should heed. We often feel that the entire world is watching and listening, especially when our feelings have been hurt. That hurt causes us to be very self-sensitive and introspective. Just walking down the street, you might feel that besides yourself, everyone else is looking at you. As common as this feeling is, it is totally unfounded. People on the street are much more concerned about their own personal situation than upon any condition besetting you. Even if some event were to draw attention to you, the attention would be short-lived and quickly forgotten. So, reassure yourself and get going. Unjust criticism should not prevent you from getting on with the job.

Summary

This chapter has addressed two very important points for improving your work performance—becoming more self-disciplined and overcoming procrastination.

Self-discipline can be improved by putting the following points into practice:

- At starting time get to your workspace and get settled.
- Define the tasks to be completed that work session.
- Divide large jobs into more manageable tasks.
- Establish realistic deadlines.
- Set specific rewards.

Overcoming procrastination can be an equally difficult task as it can be based upon quite strong fears of failure or striving for perfection. The following suggestions were discussed in the chapter:

- Remind yourself daily: I will not procrastinate today!
- Write out a daily plan each day and be certain that you start with the

really important jobs. Double check your list to make sure that you have not avoided crucial jobs.

- Attack work fears using systematic desensitisation.
- Be wary of inhibiting perfectionism.
- Work beyond unjust criticism from others.

4

Enhancing your concentration

Concentration lapses are surprisingly common. You can probably recall in the last few days a time when you thought you were working diligently, but had no recall for the details of the work being done. While these journeys into fantasy are often enjoyable and quite interesting, repeated concentration lapses at work can create difficulties. In order to appraise your powers of work concentration, read through the following checklist.

Concentration checklist

The items listed below describe a range of work-related concentration situations. Which items characterise your work habits and patterns?

- My workspace is cluttered with photos and other distracting memorabilia.
- I often look up and around to see what is of interest in my work vicinity.
- I easily nod off if working on boring tasks.
- The water cooler or coffee machine lures me from my workspace too often.
- Small and insignificant tasks often interrupt my work on important jobs.
- I ring friends or colleagues during work hours to break the monotony of my job.
- My moodiness makes it difficult for me to concentrate.
- I am frequently uncomfortable at my workspace.
- Workplace noises make me fidgety.
- I am often irritated by office politics.
- I cannot leave home problems at home—they invade my mind at work and elsewhere.

- When I am doing a difficult job, my concentration is particularly weak.
- Backbiting remarks from others at work cause me to worry and fret.

Given the frequency and prevalence of concentration problems, you have probably marked more items than you initially expected. In order to hurdle these barriers to effective work, it is important to know your own concentration obstacles. Just as in many sports, experienced competitors study the particular obstacles which must be managed during their events, astute employees are advised to do the same at their workplace. Knowing the who, what, where and when of your concentration problems will enable you to be much more definite, disciplined and diligent at work.

In assessing your workplace concentration powers, look around your immediate environment to identify potential distractors. Take special note of the people with whom you work and the physical setting—desk top distractors, your work furniture, the temperature, the location and force of air conditioners and any other aspects which have disturbed your concentration in the past or could disturb your work in the future.

Case study: Gloria

As a demonstration of how concentration can be adversely affected by personal and physical factors, let's look at the case of Gloria. Gloria was working as a secretary/telephonist in a large organisation. At a recent personnel review, her work was appraised as being unsatisfactory and she was strongly advised to improve the quality of her work. In our meeting, Gloria reported that she normally coped well with her work, but the last six months had been particularly stressful. She had exhausted her annual sick leave entitlement because of chronic headaches.

Gloria was frightened she would be dismissed if she did not improve significantly. She believed her poor concentration was due to the frequent and severe headaches, but other factors emerged. Firstly, the position of her desk was directly in front of the air conditioner which blew a steady stream of cold air across her head, neck, shoulders, and back. A second factor was the position of her typing copy. She generally placed her copy on the right-hand corner of her desk, causing her to twist her head and neck to an uncomfortable degree. One final problem was Philip, a senior employee who had the habit of frequently walking behind her to check on the accuracy of her work. These three factors summed to give her a predictable pain in the neck (plus head, shoulders, back and elsewhere) and certainly disrupted her concentration.

The solution? In Gloria's case, they were unusually simple and very effective. Gloria was advised to ask her boss if she could change the position of her desk to get away from the air conditioner's cold air stream. She came up with a new arrangement of her office area—her desk is now at the far side of the office in a protected position away from both the air conditioner and Philip. She also put in a requisition for an adjustable document holder which would hold her typing copy at eye level in front of her. Following these changes in her work situation, Gloria's headaches markedly decreased and her concentration vastly improved. With no headaches and more privacy in her work area, Gloria's work was rated as 'very satisfactory' at the end of her next evaluation period.

Gloria's case was fairly straightforward and the solutions were relatively simple. Most concentration problems, however, are far more complex and difficult, mainly because they involve poor mental discipline and often emotional, rather than rational responses to work situations. Let's look at some of these problem areas.

Building stronger and longer concentration periods

Building your concentration power is much like developing and strengthening the muscles of your body. However, you will be able to improve your concentration without working up a profuse sweat. It's more a matter of cool, calm and conscientious practice.

The basic process in developing your concentration powers is to gradually take on more difficult mental tasks. These tasks should require more rigorous and more lengthy periods of concentration. As you progress, reward yourself for increases in your concentration span.

The first step is to prepare a list of concentration tasks which you normally confront in your work or at home. If you have difficulty recalling and recounting situations where your concentration is critical or necessary, carry a notebook with you for two weeks and note the situations requiring firm concentration.

For example, you may have had difficulty at work repeating the verbal instructions of a colleague telling you how to operate a new machine. Or, you might have difficulty following travel directions on a weekend trip. After you have collected your concentration items, rank them in order from the easiest to the most difficult.

Now that you have listed and ranked your items, start with the easiest one. Let's say that it is proofreading a two-page letter to pick up any typographic mistakes. Gather together some practice material—old letters or current reports that need to be scrutinised. Set a concentration time target, say five minutes, and then get to the task. Don't look up or break your concentration in any other way. When the time is up (you might use an alarm clock), check your performance. Were you able to hold your concentration to the task? Qualitatively, were you able to pick up any errors in the letters? When you can maintain effective concentration over three separate trials at a particular time span then move up to the next level. By working at each task, beginning with relatively short concentration periods and progressing to longer time spans, you will be able to increase your work concentration appreciably.

It is important to say that fatigue is a significant factor which affects concentration. Concentrating is generally hard work. Therefore, you will want to gauge your effective concentration periods to the type of work to be done and schedule adequate rest periods to offset fatigue.

I used an approach similar to this with John, an apprentice electrician who felt he wasn't bright enough for the job he was taking on. John's supervisor was quite supportive and understanding but he was getting frustrated by John's apparent inability to follow instructions. With the supervisor's help, I suggested that a series of audio cassette tapes be prepared, starting with short and simple sets of instructions and progressing to more difficult ones. John was to play each set of instructions and then try to repeat the steps verbatim. As a concentration and memory aid, I suggested that he quickly repeat each step after it was presented and then form a mental image to help lock each step into his memory. In other words, listen, repeat, imagine, apply.

You might want to see how proficient you are at concentrating by doing the following task. Imagine that you are travelling and have become lost. Ask a friend to read the following instructions to you to see if you can concentrate, retain and then repeat the set.

Concentration practice exercise

In order to get to the Town Hall, continue down Foster Street for three blocks.

Turn right at the Catholic Church onto Cavendish Street and continue for another two blocks.

You'll see the City Garage on your left. Turn right there on to Forbes Street which takes you straight down to the Town Hall in four blocks.

It's harder than it looks initially, isn't it? Don't despair. Try the following pointers to boost your concentration:

- Take the series slowly so that you can mentally absorb each step.
- Repeat each step out loud to help fix the information in your memory.
- Ask questions to clarify any ambiguities or doubts.
- Try to establish a mental image of each step to link it with the preceding and succeeding steps (church steeples, cars at City Garage, etc.).
- At the end of the series, try to repeat the entire set of instructions. Correct any faults.
- When carrying out the instructions, repeat the steps as you go to further fix the series in your memory, if retention is necessary.

The same approach can be used to confront the vexing problem of remembering the names of people you meet, especially in groups. Your face may often flush and tingle when you are expected to introduce a person whose name you cannot recall. It's happened to all of us and silently we have said, 'I've got to do something about concentrating and remembering people's names!'

Essentially, you can follow the same principles as noted above with a few minor alterations. When being introduced to a group of people, slow the pace of the introductions by repeating each person's name out loud. Slowing the pace will allow you to fix the name of each person with some personal characteristic. For example, if you have just been introduced to Michael McGraw, a particularly large person, you might picture Michael as a giant wearing a Scottish kilt. Sounds a bit zany, but the zanier you make your images of the people, the more likely it is you will be able to connect the image with the person and the person with the correct name. It will take some practice and some creative thinking, but the system does work. If zany imagery is not your strong suit, then resort to pen and paper. Simply writing the names of new people you have met as soon as possible after meeting them plus a note or two about your connection with them will help your memory immensely.

John, a friend who has been a company representative for over 25 years, takes professional pride in remembering the names of most of the people with whom he deals or calls on. He remarked that his clients often comment upon his incredible memory for their names, as well as the names of ancillary staff and even family members. How does he do it? Fundamentally, with some hard work and diligent record keeping. Every time he calls upon a client, he fills out a card with the names of any new staff he met at the shop or store. He also notes important dates, such as the anniversary of the shop's opening, the birthday of the shop proprietor, the date of the shop's expansion, etc. It might sound contrived and somewhat false, but who doesn't like to be remembered? He's never had a complaint. In fact, his clients look forward to his visits, which are really more of a personal experience than a commercial duty.

Thus, concentration powers can be developed and improved, but the process does require some hard work and conscientious practice. Take some time each day and work on your concentration power. Use the steps suggested above and you will be surprised how quickly you will improve. As suggested earlier, the mind is just as amenable to practice effects as are your body muscles. Regular practice will produce the desired effect— stronger concentration.

There are other factors in addition to poor concentration habits which cause us to mentally wander off our work tasks. Your attitude towards your work, strong emotional reactions to people working with you, and conditions in your immediate workspace are just a few of the concentration problem sources which can affect you as a worker. Let's look briefly at these areas.

Enhancing your work attitude

People work for various reasons, but if they are not getting basic work satisfaction in the forms of stimulation, challenge, encouragement and reward, then their concentration could well suffer. We all know the difficulty of trying to put our heart into something which is just patently uninteresting, perhaps even boring. Boring tasks are part of most jobs, but these tasks must be done. If your work seems to be more boring and less stimulating and challenging than you would like, then do something actively about the situation.

- Ask yourself if you are in the right job for your skills and abilities. If you think you may not be in the most suitable job, talk with an employment counsellor about the possibility of a job change.
- If you are satisfied to stay in your job and suffer boredom daily, think about ways of adding variety to your workday: change the order of your work duties; consider a job exchange with another person in the organisation.
- Actively look for new and more effective ways to do the same chore.
- Focus upon the rewards for doing the task. Mentally reward yourself for getting through the really nasty and boring aspects of the job.
- Ask yourself how the job is benefiting you. Look for new ways that you can prosper by doing the job more quickly.
- Make the difficult parts of your job a personal challenge. Use relevant rewards and be proud of yourself for perservering to job's end.
- Break large and difficult jobs into shorter and more manageable tasks.
- Become task and time specific in your work. Keep a log of difficult jobs and the time required to complete them.

Your attitude towards your work is very important. If your concentration is still poor after you have tried the above suggestions, then you should discuss the situation with a professional psychologist or another helping professional. It may be that there are personal issues blocking your concentration, such as strong emotional reactions and worries. Try the following exercise to control strong mental and emotional reactions which disrupt your concentration.

Mental control exercise

- The problematic thought occurs.
- Close your eyes and picture a stop sign. See the sign flashing on and off in your mind.
- Say to yourself emphatically, stop! in rhythm with the stop sign flashing on.
- Clench a hand into a fist and contract the muscles as you say stop.!
- Repeat the process as often as necessary.

As suggested earlier, strong emotional reactions can be crippling. If you have been experiencing emotional upsets at work, then you are best advised to consult an experienced psychologist. It is far better to address these problems early than to wait and hope that they will go away.

Improving your workspace

Just as a poor work attitude and strong emotional reactions can erode your concentration at work, the basic conditions of your workspace can also cause concentration lapses. It is worthy of brief mention that certain factors in your physical environment can affect your concentration. Ideally, for optimal concentration your workspace should be:

- Free of loud and disturbing noises
- Physically comfortable
- Well-lit
- Well-ventilated
- As distraction-free as possible

The first four of these conditions fall more within the province of your employer. The final item, making your workspace as distraction-free as possible, is more likely to be your responsibility. Keep your desk top or work space tidy and clear of concentration disruptors. Re-arrange your work space so that you are not adversely affected by glare, strong drafts, and invasions by workmates. By re-designing your workspace, you will be pleasantly surprised at the positive change in your concentration powers.

Summary

Concentrating effectively and productively at work is a behavioural goal which will enhance your value as a worker. This chapter has discussed several ways of building strong powers of concentration, including the following:

- Listing the tasks in which you typically incur concentration lapses
- Working daily at lengthening your concentration span
- Using self-prepared taped information to practise concentrating upon work instructions
- When concentrating upon verbal messages, listening, repeating, imagining, and applying
- If your attitude about your job is negative, trying to increase the stimulation, challenge, and reward aspects of the work
- For strong emotional reactions which interfere with your concentration, taking active steps to deal with the emotions. Consulting a professional psychologist if you experience continuing difficulties
- Trying to improve the physical conditions of your workspace by dealing with disruptive noises, making your workspace comfortable and improving the lighting and ventilation

5

Increasing your confidence

Personal confidence is something most of us would like more of, but it's just a matter of generating it. How can we become more confident? Psychologists and therapists would agree that if a personal confidence pill were to be invented, the world would be a much happier place and they would quickly be out of work. But a confidence pill has yet to be produced. Where do we turn to bolster our self-confidence? Basically, into ourselves to bolster and develop low areas which need attention.

Before going further into how you can increase your confidence, it is important to define what is meant by the term. Essentially, self-confidence is a combination of thought and feeling which means, I feel good about myself and think that I am a worthwhile person. In the work sphere, the confident person generally feels positive and competent and uses these qualities to perform the job well, on time and perhaps with enthusiasm.

Being self-confident might seem ultra-difficult, especially for the pessimists, but the attitudes held about oneself can be improved. Just as in previous chapters, you will need to become aware of your present behaviours which foster non-confidence and then practise and persevere with the strategies discussed in this chapter to redress the balance.

Perhaps the case of Shane will help to illustrate the importance of self-confidence in the workplace. Shane initially sought help because of marital problems. Shane's wife had discovered that he had been having an affair. In the sessions which followed, Shane said that his marriage of six years had become dull and uninteresting and that his work was boring. He explained further, 'This lass at work showed a lot of interest in me and made me feel good.' They initially started just having coffee breaks together, but extended their liaison to drinks after work. It wasn't too long before their meetings became more involved.

While the focus of counselling was upon the marriage, considerable attention had to be addressed to Shane's level of self-confidence, both at home and at work. Because he felt negatively about himself and his work, he retreated into a state of stagnation. The longer he just survived in his job, the more confidence he lost. As part of the counselling, Shane was encouraged to enrol in a part-time technical college course to improve his qualifications. He responded enthusiastically. Soon after starting the course, he requested a transfer to another department so that he could challenge himself with new duties and responsibilities. The distress, guilt and shame which he initially experienced both at work and at home soon became replaced by a determined drive to improve himself. Thirteen months after he commenced counselling as a shameful and shattered individual, he radiated a healthy exuberance. His bolstered confidence made him more courageous and determined to succeed, both in his work and in his marriage.

While Shane is but one person who improved his self-confidence, this chapter will present strategies which may well be of help to a wider range of people—perhaps you. You can learn how to break free from negative thoughts and feelings, to become more positive and confident. More specifically, the chapter will focus upon: monitoring and managing negative thinking; promoting more positive thoughts about yourself; taking reasonable and calculated risks; and becoming more assertive.

Monitoring negative thinking

Negative thinking is, unfortunately, very common. As you will most likely agree, being negative is not a desirable characteristic for success-bound employees. How negative are you about your work? For example, do you typically:

- Spend large amounts of time worrying about your inadequacies?
- Defer to other workmates when you know you can speak competently on an important issue at a meeting?
- Hold back from submitting a major project because you think it's not good enough?
- Compare yourself to others and always come out on the losing side?
- Choose not to make waves in potentially difficult situations?

These items paint a very negative picture, don't they? Before this negativity gets too entrenched, let's focus upon what can be done about it. For starters, why not check yourself to see how frequently you are thinking or feeling negatively? As suggested in earlier chapters, it's helpful to carry a notebook with you and when you catch yourself thinking or feeling negatively, then jot down some notes about the situation. Use the following headings to monitor your negative thoughts and feelings.

Log of negative thoughts and feelings

Where? _____
When? _____
With whom? _____
Why? _____

The first three headings will be easy to complete. However, the why? question may pose some problems. You might know that you're feeling off and very negative, but there might be no apparent cause or reason. Instead of leaving a blank, try guessing, as guesses give at least some information.

Having monitored your thoughts and feelings for a week or two, read your notes and see if there are any trends. At this point it is necessary to say that if your notebook was filled by day three or four and you continued to feel grey to black for the remaining period, you may want to seek professional advice. Your local doctor or a clinical psychologist will be interested to review your notes to learn more about your daily feelings and thoughts.

Assuming that there is no psychopathology (that is, you are essentially well, but have the occasional negative episode), then you may well want to know what can be done about your negativity.

Managing negative thoughts and feelings

Most people, if given the choice between positive or negative thoughts, would choose the former. In the context of the present chapter, that's the proper choice, but what do you do about the negative residue? Here are some suggestions about how you can manage negative thoughts and feelings.

- Use the stop sign technique. Briefly, whenever you find yourself thinking negatively and you wish to get on with your work, focus your mind upon a stop sign. As you spell the letters s-t-o-p to yourself, clench a hand into a fist and contract the muscles as you spell each letter and say the word, stop! to yourself. The visual, auditory and tactile stimuli which preoccupy your mind will displace effectively the negative thought or feeling. Repeat the process as often as necessary.

- Stand up or turn away from your workspace when your work is affected by negative thinking. Do not allow yourself to be worrying and fretting unnecessarily while trying to get on with your work.

- Keep a worry list. Some worries are worth worrying about, so write them down and spend some time after work reviewing the list and thinking constructively about solutions. By keeping such a list, trivial worries will be given short shrift and you will find yourself saying, Don't be silly! It's ridiculous worrying about that!

- Do something about worries which are realistically based. Think creatively and laterally, entertaining a range of possible solutions. Read De Bono's books on creative problem solving to help overcome these worries.

- If you find that some negative thoughts have no possible solution (Most of my workmates are taller than I am.), then ban the thought from your mind and replace it with a more positive one. See the next section for some suggestions.

- Chart the frequency of your negative thinking. As you go through your workday, make a mark in a notebook every time you think negatively. At the end of the day, simply count the number of marks and chart them on a graph. Work diligently at trying to get the graph to go down—that is, work at thinking negatively less frequently.

- Reward yourself for working through days in which you have had less frequent negative thoughts and/or feelings.

- If your negative thoughts and feelings persist, see your doctor or a clinical pyschologist.

In essence, then, negative thinking can be an irksome and counter-productive habit which can undermine your work effectiveness. Just as you learned this habit, you can un-learn it. Counting and charting your negative thoughts will decrease the frequency of these work interruptors and taking time for creative problem solving should help you to eliminate some from the worry list.

Promoting positive thinking

Having learned how to un-learn the habit of thinking and feeling negatively, let's look at how you can now replace the former negative experiences with more positive ones. For convenience, imagine yourself starting your workday, then being at work, and finally leaving work at the end of the day. Read the following suggestions and see if some of the points might apply to help you to become a more positive person, prior to, during and after work.

Before work:

- On waking each workday, think about the most interesting and exciting part of the forthcoming day. Do not accept the response, 'Nothing!'.
- Before getting out of bed, say something to yourself like, 'I will make the most of my abilities today!'.
- When dressing, consider wearing clothing which is different—something which may evoke positive remarks and compliments from workmates. A positive remark can put some brightness into a grey day.
- Plan a positive experience each day and then look forward to it.
- Eat a healthy and hearty breakfast so that you have the energy to make the most of the day.
- If you drive to work, repeat a positive saying at each red traffic light. For example, 'I can complete the James report today!', assuming that this is a realistic and achievable task.
- When you arrive at work, pause briefly before entering your workplace, take a comfortably deep breath, relax as you breathe out and then enter with a relaxed and positive bearing.

At work:

- On entering your workplace, greet your workmates with a pleasant 'Hello' or 'Nice day' (or, 'Rotten day out there, isn't it?').

- Take a few minutes to have a brief chat with particular workmates, as the occasion warrants.
- When you get to your workspace, get settled straight away and write out your daily plan.
- Make certain that you get right to your high priority tasks.
- Look forward to the pleasant event(s) which you have scheduled during the day.
- Reward yourself for having completed your first significant task of the day by telling a close workmate about the accomplishment.
- Participate actively in meetings.
- Use your coffee breaks and lunch break to meet with workmates whose company you enjoy.
- If time allows, try to get out of your workplace for a brisk and vigorous walk after lunch.
- Survey the availability of pleasant places nearby where you can take your lunch and get some exercise as well.
- Keep updating your daily plan as you complete tasks or as new tasks occur during the day.
- Tell a close workmate how the day is going for you.
- When meeting with your boss or supervisor, be certain to provide a relevant and brief commentary about your progress on any special projects.
- Consider expanding your circle of friends at work. Invite a newcomer at work to join your group at the coffee break or at lunch.
- At the end of the day, review your daily plan, taking special note of the crossed off jobs. Take pride in your accomplishments. If there are outstanding tasks, place them on the plan for tomorrow.
- Clear your workspace so that you can get right down to work when you arrive tommorrow.

After work:

- Occasionally, join your workmates after work for a drink or chat so as to keep in touch socially as well as vocationally.
- As a special treat, buy some flowers or another small gift on your way home. You, your spouse or housemate(s) can

enjoy the celebration of Wednesday or any other day, just because it is that particular day.

- Discuss the high points and the low points of your day with your spouse or housemates. Ask their opinion about any specific problems you might be having at work and be certain to reciprocate.

- During the after work hours, try to go out and get some vigorous exercise to blow off any accumulated tensions from the day. Just a brisk thirty minute walk will do wonders for you.

- Make ample provision for time with your family and close friends during evenings and weekends. These important support people can play a most significant part in maintaining a positive and productive outlook in your work life.

- Get to bed in time to have a full night's rest. Insufficient sleep can be a problem for very busy people and irritability and crankiness can result. See Chapter 7 for suggestions about how to calm your mind and body so sleep can come.

Thus, you can make your work life and your personal life much more positive by starting your days with a positive outlook and reinforcing this approach during and after work. Taking time to think positively about yourself and those close to you will help you overcome many obstacles. Some obstacles, however, may cause you to step back. The next section addresses the topic of being more assertive in your work.

Advancing assertively

For people at work, assertiveness has particularly important significance, as it is a quality which helps you to communicate more effectively and hopefully achieve your goals. Gail, an administrative assistant with a large multi-national company, had been feeling she deserved a promotion after performing quietly, but well in her position for two and a half years. She had the ability to advance, but she loathed the interviewing and assessments to which she would be subjected when her application was being considered. She was also very aware that she often deferred to others when in discussions, even though she had a worthwhile point to put forward. We met for twelve sessions over a six month period and Gail worked daily on various assertiveness exercises. Her hard work won her the promotion.

Roger's case points out another aspect of assertiveness. He was well-regarded by his workmates and was known as an ever-willing person who wouldn't say No to others. However, some of his workmates took advantage of his willing nature. Even though Roger's desk was generally piled high with work, he was often asked to do various jobs to help out others. These requests were pleasantly put to Roger and he found himself saying Yes. As he worked after hours to complete his own work, he became hostile and angry—not necessarily at his workmates, but at himself because he wasn't able to refuse their requests. One day, Roger's anger exploded in the office. He was referred to me for counselling.

The cases of Gail and Roger exemplify the plight of many workers. It is very important to be able to stand and be heard, whether the situation is a promotion interview or a refusal to an unfair request. To remain silent under these circumstances can create strong feelings of anger inside and erode the individual's self-confidence. Some other situations which often require assertiveness at the workplace are:

- Communicating your thoughts and feelings directly and honestly.
- Saying, Yes to new work opportunities and possibilities which you wish to try.
- Giving compliments to others.
- Receiving compliments from others.
- Dealing effectively with reprimands.

Having listed some assertiveness situations which might be relevant to you, how can you go about becoming more assertive? Perhaps the following five steps will help to fix the process in your mind and assist you in putting the process into action:

Step 1   *Plan your words and actions*

Having sensed that your rights are being infringed in a particular situation, think through what you will say and do when you are next in the situation. Keep your statement short and to the point and use appropriate gestures, eye contact and other body language to emphasise what you are saying. For example, 'Mr. James, I feel annoyed that I am always asked to do the photocopying for others when it is really not part of my job.'

Step 2 *Ponder the other person's response*

Think how your message is going to affect the other person and how they will then respond. Step into their shoes and see and hear yourself from their perspective. Make any readjustments to your planned approach.

Step 3 *Practise your message*

Even if you are actually in the confrontation, take a brief pause to run through mentally what you will say and how you will say it. If you have more time, try practising your message while looking into a mirror so you can see and hear yourself as you will be perceived by the other person.

Step 4 *Perform!*

Having planned, pondered and practised your response, now perform. Don't hesitate or procrastinate, do it! Yes, it does take courage, but once you have learned the fine art of being more assertive, you will not regret your actions.

Step 5 *Perfect your performance*

The chief benefit from trying something new is that you have the opportunity of learning from your experience. Even if your first attempt is not successful—perhaps even an outright failure—look back upon the experience and identify the aspects which can be improved. Practice will make a difference.

By becoming more assertive, you are off to a new quality in your worklife. Speak out honestly (but tactfully) and directly when you sense that your rights are being infringed. As stated above, your early attempts are likely to be learning trials, but don't lose hope or drive. Keep at it and try that much harder. If you become disenchanted, speak with a clincial psychologist who is skilled in communication training. Some additional help will soon get you back on to a positive and more confident course.

Summary

This chapter has covered various approaches to the very important and basic issue of being more confident in the workplace and with your work effort. The following topics were discussed and practical guidelines were suggested:

- Monitoring your negative thinking
- Keeping a log of your negative thoughts and feelings
- Managing negative thoughts and feelings
  The 'stop sign' technique
  Keeping a 'worry list'
  Using creative thinking to solve problems
  Charting your frequency of negative thoughts
- Promoting more positive thinking
- Advancing assertively
  Plan your words and actions
  Ponder the response possibilities
  Practise your assertive approach
  Perform
  Perfect your performance

6

Boosting your productivity

How often do you ...

( ) Dawdle before work, causing frequent lateness?
( ) Forget things?
( ) Fidget around losing productive work time?
( ) Misunderstand instructions?
( ) Take extended coffee breaks?
( ) Get major assignments and projects in late?
( ) Feel at odds with your boss?
( ) Feel alienated from your workmates?
( ) Take sick leave when you are feeling 'just a bit off'?
( ) Daydream about being elsewhere than at work?

The items above suggest a common picture—the non-productive worker. Of course, we all have bad days and even the occasional disastrous period, but if non-productive events crop up regularly in your day-to-day work, then you should do something about them. If you don't, your boss might.

Being productive is what most jobs are all about. Productivity means that you are doing what is expected—getting the job done. Aside from fulfilling the expectations of your employer, being productive is also one of the major elements in job satisfaction. By working hard and accomplishing your set goals, you feel more fulfilled at the end of the day.

This chapter will discuss several important aspects of productivity ranging from personal issues such as understanding and satisfying your personal needs in your work life to various ways of boosting your productivity. Having discussed these issues, the chapter will end with a productivity problem clinic focusing upon the problems of job burn out, absenteeism, boredom at work, and problems with your boss.

Understanding your work needs

One of the most common reasons for low productivity is that workers' needs are not being met on the job. Non-productive workers will often claim they are frustrated in or alienated by their jobs. Let's look briefly at several examples.

Paul, a friend who loved the piano, was pushed into studying medicine by his family because there was no future or security in playing the piano. After graduating from medical school, Paul persisted with medicine because he was too old at that stage to go back and pursue a career as a concert pianist. Even though the financial rewards in medicine were encouraging, Paul was not really satisfied in his work. Basically, he just was not interested in working with sick people. His heart was really with music and the piano. He solved his problem by working only part-time as an industrial medicine consultant and devoting the remainder of the working week to music. He was fortunate to have the finance and time to pursue his true love.

Betty, a secretary in a large organisation, disliked the impersonal feeling of being a five-digit number in a multi-national computer company. She far preferred working amongst people who were 'on the same wavelength'. After three years, she left her secretarial work and started her own business as an interior designer. With this fairly radical change, she found new satisfactions and far more interest in her new work.

Bill, a factory foreman, was becoming increasingly dissatisfied at work. More and more pressure was being placed upon him due to a recent takeover of the company. He found himself in conflict between his work team and the new high pressure management. In order to cope more effectively with the new situation, he asked for special leave to attend an external course on assertiveness training and supervisory skills. One returning to work, he found that his new approach to management instilled vigour and vitality to his work life.

These brief sketches show how personal issues can limit your work productivity. The sketches also point out the necessity to take strong and deliberate action to sort out low productivity problems. If you are not working productively in your job, you may either improve your situation, leave and do something else, or continue in your existing rut.

Before you consider making any major changes, take time to

appraise your personal qualities so you have a better understanding of how your needs might be more satisfactorily met either in your present job or in another line of work. You may well benefit from speaking with a professional psychologist about your work needs. Career counselling can be a most helpful experience if your productivity is marginal or lapsing. The counselling process could well involve some psychological testing of your aptitudes and vocational skills. You can get a brief overview of some of the relevant issues from the questions below.

Personal needs at work

- Do you prefer to work in a small business, a large organisation, or on your own?
- Do you enjoy initiating new developments and seeing them fulfilled in your work?
- How important are workplace friendships? Do you rely upon these daily contacts to provide interest and stimulation to your work day?
- Are you competitive? Do you like pushing yourself and comparing your achievements with others?
- Are you a creative person who needs to express yourself frequently in your work?
- Do you see yourself as a leader? Do you enjoy exercising control over your situation at work and delegating responsibilities to others?
- What sorts of rewards are important to you? High salary; status in the job title; fringe benefits (car, expenses); long-term security etc.
- How willing are you to take risks, to try even though you know there is a considerable chance of failure?
- Do you prefer to work: inside or outside; with people, ideas, or equipment?

The profile, although brief, should cause you to think analytically and constructively about the type of person you are. It is perfectly possible that you have not been working as productively as possible because your job is not fulfilling some basic personal needs. What can you do about this situation? Read on.

Satisfying your work needs

As suggested above, productive workers tend to satisfy their personal work needs in their job. That is, they usually strive to further their goals because they like what they do. Becoming more satisfied at work can be a complex problem, but try the following suggestions.

A very important aspect of work productivity is recognition. When you and your work do not get desired recognition from your boss and others, productivity can suffer. If work recognition and rewards are low or lacking, talk to your boss about the problem. Bosses should be very aware of the importance of positive feedback, but some have difficulty giving this important type of reinforcement.

Look back upon the positive and productive experiences you have had in your work life. Did you enjoy seeing personal projects carried through to completion? Was the job challenging and stimulating? Were you working with compatible others, and if so, what type of people did your particularly enjoy? Knowing what was satisfying in the past is likely to help make your work more satisfying in the future.

Give some thought to your long-term plans, both reality-based and fantasy. It is quite easy to get bogged down in the hum drum and banal events of day-to-day work. Think ahead and consider your future. Positive long-term goals can offer some inducement to press ahead with more vivacity and vigour in your present situation.

A friend, Tom, was just coping with his managerial job. He admitted that he was trapped in his position by his age and his house mortgage. However, he dreamed of the day when he could take his retirement pay and invest in a small garden nursery business, a dream which sustained his drive and productivity at his present job. Whether his plan ever eventuates remains to be seen, but the goal goads him on, especially on his down days.

Jennifer also experienced a growing disenchantment with her job. She had been working as a staff accountant for a large bank and, after fourteen years, there were very few surprises left in the job. She wanted to stay with the bank because of her comfortable salary and the advantageous home loan she enjoyed, but she desperately needed a change. She spoke with the personnel manager about her situation and a transfer to the money market department was suggested. The transfer sounded a bit frightening, but it was a new and exciting challenge and Jennifer accepted. She found her new work in the money market to be much more fulfilling than she had anticipated and after six months, she has no plans to return to orthodox accounting. Thus, transferring within the organisation to a new and more challenging job can be a very productive and propitious step forward.

Making a move to a new department generally requires a positive attitude, an attribute which is all too frequently in short supply in many workers. Regrettably, many people dwell upon the negatives of their work life. Their conversation overflows with complaints, dissatisfactions and other gripes and groans. However, with a bit of encouragement, most people can nominate at least a few positive experiences in their past work careers. Take some time periodically and write down a list of the positive things you are getting from your work. You might think that the list will be very short, but sit down with a friend or colleague and discuss the issue. You will probably be surprised to find that your work provides more pleasure than you initially thought.

Thus, feeling disenchanted and non-productive in your work life can be a frequent event, but one which can and should be addressed. If you cannot see a way out of a low productivity work problem, read on.

Enhancing productivity

While jobs vary in work tasks and objectives, there are some general and basic procedures which can be implemented to enhance worker productivity.

- Work to a daily plan as described in Chapter 1.
- Look for ways in which you can productively use previously unused time.
- Start a follow-up file to periodically contact people who are important to your work. Be certain to record background information, special events and possibly even important birthdays on your file cards.
- Practise placing yourself in the shoes of the people you deal with and see yourself from their perspective. Can you approach them more positively? Can you make them feel more positive in their relationship with you?

- Talk with experienced people in your field of work and try the strategies they used to increase their productivity.
- Update your job skills.

Thus, your productivity can be enhanced by understanding yourself and your work needs. Address these needs so that your work becomes a satisfying and positive experience. If satisfactions appear to be unattainable, then consider changing jobs or career. Before jumping into a major change, consider the problem clinic below to see if the problems and solutions described have direct relevance to your situation.

Productivity problem clinic

This section addresses some basic problems at work which can hamper productivity, including job burn out, absenteeism, boredom and problems with your boss. These problems are not mutually exclusive, but let's look at each in turn.

Burning out

Considerable attention has been given recently to the topic of job burn out, or in more orthodox terms, going stale in your job. People burn out when they no longer experience challenge nor derive satisfaction from their work.

What can be done about the burn out problem? Here are a few suggestions.

- Take rest breaks throughout the working day and practise relaxing physically, mentally and emotionally.
- Investigate a job exchange or special leave to update your skills.
- Be certain to take periodic holidays. Resist the temptation to stockpile your recreation leave.
- Maintain close relations with other workers to discuss common work problems and to obtain peer support.
- Make your job as varied as possible. Avoid work ruts where every hour of your day becomes entirely predictable.
- Maintain active involvement in your outside interests and hobbies to give some diversity and excitement to your life.
- Talk about your feelings, both good and bad, with close

friends at work and your family. Don't store up strong
emotions.
- If you begin to suffer from vague illnesses, poor sleep and
disrupted relationships with colleagues and friends, talk with
a psychologist about your experiences at work. Be certain to
mention any present dissatisfactions.

Thus, burn out is a very real condition which can decrease your
productivity at work. However, you can take specific steps to
prevent yourself from burning out. Put into practice the points
noted above. If you have questions about your physical or
emotional health in respect to your work life, discuss the situation
with a psychologist or your doctor.

Absenteeism

Absenteeism continues to be a major industrial and economic
problem. The causes are numerous, but where worker satisfaction
is high, absenteeism is generally low. The problem is all too
frequently dismissed by workers as a fault with the system, but
management generally takes a far more serious view. Absent
workers put a strain on their workmates who are generally
required to take over the duties of the missing person. With less
than the required number of workers available, the work process
can be significantly retarded causing serious declines in productivity.
  If you, the worker, are aware that you are taking time off work
for sickies or because you are feeling just a bit off, then you should
ask yourself what is wrong with your work situation. What is
prompting you to be absent when you are basically fit for work?
We can all have grey to black days. However, if these days occur
every week or so, there is a problem somewhere.
  Finding the cause of the absenteeism problem might be surprisingly difficult. Sometimes we bury issues deeply inside because
they pose strong and serious threats to our confidence or self-
esteem. If you think there is a problem and you can not identify it,
talk to a close friend who knows you well, to a family member, to
your doctor or to a psychologist. It is important to realise that
being inappropriately absent from work can be a sign that something is wrong—in the way that body pain tells us our body is not
functioning correctly. Don't ignore the problem and hope that it
will go away—do something about it.

If you don't address the problem, your boss might. Hopefully your boss has your best interests at heart (as well as the interests of the organisation). If your boss raises the issue with you, take the opportunity to discuss the situation. There could be a solution available which you haven't considered. Discuss plans which will encourage reliable work attendance. Additionally, deal with work issues which might be contributing to absenteeism, such as boredom.

Boredom

A frequent work problem which is often associated with absenteeism is boredom. Most jobs have their repetitive and boring aspects which simply must be done. However, your attitude about these less than stimulating tasks is paramount. Do you linger, loiter and lounge about before getting to the task? Or, do you say to yourself, 'Yes, this is a boring task, but it must be done. Better get to it and get it over with!' The latter approach might seem idealistic, but some variation on the theme can help you get to and through the boring aspects of your job. Let's look at some other suggestions which you might implement to decrease boredom at work.

- Take an active role in policy and decision-making if possible.
- Ask your boss for more responsibility in your job.
- Look for new challenges, new approaches to your job.
- Maintain close relations with your workmates and discuss any work-related frustrations.
- Investigate the possibility of job-sharing, mixed duties, temporary secondment to another section and other plans to bring new stimulation to your job.
- Attend work-related educational courses to update your skills.
- If you have complaints, put them to your boss and the management. Many complaints have been the seed of positive and productive innovations at work, especially where management teams have been alert and sensitive to workers' issues.
- Make a list of the people in management who have shown an active interest in your work. If you think no-one is in-

terested, discuss this with the management—it is a problem which they should address.

- Plan rewards for achieving specific targets at work. Focus on these rewards as an inducement to get through the boring tasks.
- Prepare an official citation which you can present to yourself and to other colleagues for 'perseverence and persistence in the face of absolute boredom'. Humour can make boredom more tolerable and transient.

Thus, every job will have its boring tasks, but your attitude towards these boring aspects is very important. Confront boredom firmly and positively and get through the tasks quickly and effectively. Boredom will exist as long as you remain passive and inactive. Attack the problem (not your boss!) and try to limit the boredom problem.

Problems with your boss

In terms of your advancement, promotion (or stagnation) and general welfare at work, the most important person outside of yourself is your boss. The relationships between bosses and their employees can be: close to distant, warm to cool, authoritarian to democratic, and open to closed, to name but a few relevant dimensions.

An entire book could be devoted to the complexities of the boss-worker relationships, but there are two aspects which the worker would be well-advised to foster—trust and respect.

Trust, in the context of your relationship with your boss, essentially means that you can be trusted to carry out your duties effectively and on time. It also implies that you will be loyal to the organisation and to your boss. In operational terms, you can be given a task to do and you will accept the responsibility for seeing that it gets done. From the boss' perspective, trust in you means less need for worry about the job getting done.

Respect is an equally important consideration. Your boss will respect you for the work you do if it is done well. It is perfectly possible for your boss not to like you, but still respect you and your work. Of course, it is preferable to be liked and respected, but given that this is a problem clinic section, we will focus upon the negative side of the issue. What can you do to win your boss' respect? Here are some pointers.

- Be enthusiastic about your job. Do your best each day.
- Be conscientious. Do a fair day's work for your pay.
- Be dependable. Get your work done on time.
- Be innovative. Look for ways in which you can improve yourself and your work.
- Be willing to accept additional responsibilities within your range of competency. Your boss may wish to delegate new duties to encourage growth at your job.
- Be aware of your limitations. If you are in doubt about your capabilities to perform a set task, ask for appropriate assistance.
- Be flexible and adaptable. If an urgent work matter arises or if overtime is requested, be co-operative.

The boss and your workmates will respect you and your competencies if you can demonstrate most of these qualities. If these objectives seem unattainable to you, observe co-workers for whom your boss has respect. What is your colleague doing to earn that respect? We live in a human laboratory and valuable lessons can be learned every day from those around us. Careful observation can make each day a step forward in managing your boss more constructively.

Summary

Increasing your productivity at work is very important for you and the organisation for which you work. By maximising your productivity, you are more likely to achieve greater personal satisfaction from your work. Hopefully, your organisation will give you just rewards and recognition for your positive contributions. This chapter has addressed the following issues which can help you to achieve greater productivity at work:

- Understanding your present work needs
- Satisfying your work needs
- Employing positive procedures to enhance your productivity
- Dealing with specific productivity problems:
    Job burn out
    Absenteeism
    Boredom at work
    Problems with your boss

7

Learning how to relax

At work, do you ...

( ) Experience frequent heart palpitations (fast and heavy beats)?
( ) Feel queasy and jittery for no explicable reason?
( ) Have difficulty concentrating because of intrusive thoughts?
( ) Worry frequently about trivial issues?
( ) Have diarrhoea frequently?
( ) Get butterflies in your stomach over insignificant things?
( ) Miss opportunities or lose time because you can't make up your mind?
( ) Pace or fidget excessively?
( ) Frequently sweat while just sitting and thinking?
( ) Have your friends asking if anything is wrong because of your withdrawn behaviour?

You will probably have personally experienced some of the above items in your work life. Just getting to and from work can accelerate your heart and breathing rates. If you face regular stress at work such as demanding deadlines, friction with your boss or co-workers, irritating customers or irksome tasks, then you can benefit from daily relaxation practice.

Learning how to relax mentally and physically

The focus of attention in the relaxation procedure is to teach you how you can effectively relax your mind. The human mind is a very active organ and, for most people, the activity is beneficial. However, there are times when this activity can impede your performance. One such time is when worry and mental restlessness prevent you from concentrating upon your work.

Learning how to relax the mind is surprisingly difficult, primarily because most people have spent little or no time learning how to quiet the mind. It is important to emphasise that relaxation training is a long-term project. That is, months of practice will be necessary to achieve the full effect. Don't be put off by the word practice because relaxation is a most pleasant and enjoyable experience. But it will take time. The following steps will be a helpful guide in learning the skill.

Practise every day

Make relaxation practice part of your daily routine. The more you practise, the better the result. Even though learning how to relax might sound simple, it's not. You'll have to practise the skill regularly and conscientiously to be able to relax whenever you wish.

How much should I practise each day? At the start of your training, several short (three to five minutes) sessions will be helpful. At this stage, longer sessions are likely to give you practice in worrying or daydreaming. As you become more skilled in controlling the activity of your mind, increase the length of the sessions. Ultimately, try to practise for about thirty minutes each day, in two fifteen-minute sessions.

One word of warning! On very busy days, you may be tempted to put off your practice sessions altogether. These are the very days when it is important to relax. So, stick to your routine and turn your mind off to the pressures of the day. In addition to giving you valuable practice and a well-needed rest, the time spent relaxing is also establishing firm personal discipline, a most important quality for ambitious workers.

Expect to relax

It is important that you develop a positive expectation that you will relax. There is little use in shouting to yourself, 'RELAX, dammit, RELAX!!' You might try instead saying calmly and decisively: 'I am going to relax now.' Relaxation is a passive process. Trying too hard will only complicate the procedure. Just sit back and let it happen.

Find a quiet place

You can relax just about anywhere, assuming you can remain undisturbed for a few minutes. If you are at home or in an office, take the telephone off the hook. If others might call in on you, place a do not disturb sign on your door. Better yet, tell them you are practising your relaxation skills before you start.

Many people have found practising on commuter buses and trains perfectly satisfactory. Others practise in their cars or stretched out on a comfortable spot in a park. The important point is to make certain that you fit the practice into your daily schedule. If you can practise at the same time and place every day, so much the better. Before long, you will find yourself anticipating the relaxation period every day.

Make yourself comfortable

As implied in the previous step, you really don't need special conditions in which to practise relaxation. You can sit on a chair, lie on a bed (caution: set an alarm in case you fall asleep, as beds carry the further expectation of going to sleep), or stretch out in a comfortable spot outside. A commuter with whom I have worked even practised while standing up on crowded trains, a difficult challenge! At the beginning of your practice session, loosen any tight clothing, unfasten tight shoelaces and remove glasses if they are heavy. Maximise your comfort. If you find yourself falling asleep in your early practice sessions, try a different setting. Sitting in a straight-backed kitchen chair in a quiet location might help you concentrate more successfully upon the procedure.

Focus upon your breathing

To start, close your eyes and focus your attention upon your breathing. Listen to the soft whistling sound as the air flows in and flows out. Be sure that you are belly breathing—your belly should be moving in and out as you breathe.

After about a minute or two of concentrating on your breathing, start counting sequentially from one to ten as you inhale and saying to yourself, RELAX as you exhale. For example, on the first inhalation, say ONE and see the number one being drawn in your mind. On exhalation, say RELAX and see the word RE--L-A-X-X-X... in your mind. Continue the counting process until you feel quiet and your mind is focused and undisturbed by intruding thoughts.

When your mind is actively occupied with the number sequence and saying, RELAX, then it will be difficult for other thoughts to distract you. Ultimately, just saying the word, RELAX, will evoke the relaxation response in you, but for the present it will be necessary to go further.

Relaxing your muscles

Systematically relaxing your muscles will help you to move more deeply into a relaxation response. Try the following approach.

Focus upon your forehead muscles, just above your eyebrows. Feel them become loose, ... warm ... heavy ... and relaxed. Now down to your eyebrows, ... very relaxed. Your cheeks and mouth muscles, ... very loose, ... very relaxed. Your jaw muscles, ... nice and loose, letting your lower jaw drop open if it wishes. Now your neck muscles, front and back; letting them become warm, ... loose, ... and very relaxed. Now let your shoulders drop as much as they want ... Notice how good it feels to let that tension go.

Now relax your arms, both of them together. Feel the tension flowing in waves down your arms and out through your fingers. Your arms feel more loose and relaxed with each breath out. Now your back muscles. Feel them sinking down ... and down into the chair (bed, grass) ... Just further and further down, ... down ... down ... More and more relaxed ... Now focus upon your chest muscles. Feel them become more loose and relaxed with each breath out. That's it, very relaxed. And now, your abdominal muscles. Letting the tension go, more and more relaxed with each breath out. Very relaxed, ... warm and relaxed. And finally, your legs. Just let the tension flow down and away, leaving your legs very loose, ... very relaxed. That's it, very relaxed.

And now, the entire body. Letting any residual muscle tension go. Feeling very relaxed. Very, ... very re-lax-x--x--ed. Quiet, ... calm ... and ... re-lax-x--x--ed.

If you are still with me and not nodding or snoring in a very relaxed stupour, I should add just one more technique. One of the major reasons why rigid and inflexible relaxation programs fail is that the user becomes bored. The more variety you can put into your relaxation practice, the greater your motivation to continue practising is likely to be. Try the following scenes as attention focusing techniques.

Focus your attention

Focusing your attention might sound easy, but it can be quite difficult, especially for the person with a very active mind. The counting series and the muscle relaxation approaches will start you on the way, but you may well need further assistance to get your mind relaxed. Try one or more of the following scenes. Make the scenes as real as possible, experiencing as many of the sensual aspects as you can.

Walk through an English garden

I am standing on a small hill overlooking a garden below on a warm and sunny day in early summer. I can feel the sun's warmth on my forehead and cheeks. On the level below, there is a lovely garden bathed in deep verdant green and punctuated by numerous flower beds filled with summer flowers. The garden is inviting and I walk over to the marble staircase which leads down to the garden.

Starting at the top step, I step down to the next and with each successive step, I can feel myself becoming more and more relaxed. Stepping now down to 18 ... 17 (feeling the smooth, cool marble under my bare feet) ... 16 ... 15 ... (counting slowly as I exhale) ... 14 ... (feeling more and more relaxed) ... 13 ... 12 ... 11 ... 10 ... (down and down) ... 9 ... 8 ... (deeper and deeper) ... 7 ... 6 ... 5 ... (very deep now) ... 4 ... 3 ... 2 ... and 1 ...

Down at the bottom of the steps, I can feel the warm, soft grass under my feet and I can smell the sweet fragrance of the summer flowers hanging heavily in the air. I walk over to a garden statue of a Grecian goddess and touch the smooth surface of the stone. Very smooth with soft flowing lines. It seems that the sun's rays penetrate the marble and meet somewhere inside the smoky white stone.

Further along in the garden, I come to one of the numerous flower beds with flowers of every colour and hue. Standing in front of a circular bed, I can hear bees buzzing from flower to flower. There are several butterflies moving about the blossoms. The fragrance is very sweet and strong. I can smell the perfume as I feel occasional soft puffs of warm air brushing against the left side of my face.

I approach a large fountain which is spraying fine jets of water into the air. I can hear the splashing and spattering of water as I approach. The mist from the spraying jets is picked up by the breeze and I can now feel the fine droplets landing on my face. Very cooling, while my face feels quite warm from the sun. The sun's rays create a vivid rainbow with intense colours of red ... orange ... yellow ... green ... blue ... and violet.

Further along in the garden, I come to a large lake with two swans, one black and one white, drifting so peacefully and effortlessly in unison. They glide through lily pads with white, pink and mauve coloured flowers. So quiet, tranquil and relaxing. Very, very relaxing.

I sit down on the bank of the lake and then lie back on the soft, warm grass. So comfortable and quiet. I can feel the warmth of the sun softly penetrating my entire body. So relaxed, very relaxed. As I lie there, I am quite alone and free from problems and concerns. Just me, warm and relaxed, alone and quiet by the lake. Very quiet, very tranquil and very calm ...

At this point you would progress to the next step in the procedure. However, an alternate scene will be presented for those who suffer from hayfever or pollen allergies or for those who simply do not like gardens, lakes, or swans.

South Pacific island beach

You have gone on a holiday to a remote South Pacific island where all of your needs are catered for. Today, I have walked to a distant beach, far removed from any habitation. I am standing at the back of the beach in the shade of some palm trees. I can hear the chirping of birds overhead and the rustling of the palm fronds as they move in the gentle wind. Looking out across the golden-white sands of the beach, I can see the blue-green water of the ocean. Glancing further out to sea, the water becomes a rich, intense blue before ending in the gentle arc of the horizon. Overhead, one large, puffy white cloud drifts slowly across the sky.

As the day is warm, I decide to go down to the water and step out from the shade of the palm trees. I can feel the warmth of the sand radiating up through the soles of my feet into my legs, ... my abdomen, ... my chest, ... arms, ... neck, ... and head. So warm, so pleasant. As I walk, almost in slow motion down to the water, I can feel the sand slowly giving way under my feet. The sand is very soft and fine.

I come to the smooth, cool sand, left damp by the receding tide. The sand is firm but receptive to my footsteps which leave their mark as I walk. I now walk to the water's edge and then into the water to calf-depth. The water is pleasantly brisk and very refreshing. I look down into the crystalline clear water and can see on the bottom several fragments of broken shell, a large star fish with purple and blue encrustations on its upper surface. I can see two small crabs scurrying away from me and a small school of silvery fish darting hither and thither. The water is so clean and clear. I scoop up several handfuls and splash it over my body. Very cool and refreshing.

I now walk back up on to the dry sand and stretch out on my beach towel, face upwards. I can feel the penetrating warmth from the sand working its way up into my back. I can feel droplets of water slowly running off the upper surface of my body. The sun warms and dries my body. So warm ... so pleasant ....

Lying on the beach, I can hear the gentle lapping of the waves upon the sand. Occasionally, a sea gull calls as it flies overhead, but apart from these sounds, it is blissfully quiet. So quiet, so calm, ... so relaxing ...

At this point you progress to the next step of the series.

Walking down to your relaxation room

Imagine yourself at the top of a lovely curving staircase. You can see the carpet flowing down and around to the left. You can feel the deep pile of the soft carpet under your bare feet. Your hand is resting upon a smooth wooden bannister. As you descend the stairs, one at a time, you will find yourself feeling more and more relaxed with each step down.

Now starting at the top, the twentieth step, you step down to 19 ... now down to 18 ... letting your hand slide down the bannister as you go ... 17 ... more relaxed with each step down ... 16 ... 15 ... 14 ... 13 ... feeling the soft carpet under your feet ... 12 ... 11 ... 10 ... relaxed, more and more relaxed ... 9 ... 8 ... 7 ... more relaxed with each breath out ... 6 ... 5 ... 4 ... very relaxed now, very relaxed ... 3 ... 2 ... and now, down to 1 ... very, very relaxed.

Across the landing at the bottom of the stairs you see a large, very thick door which leads into your private room. You walk over to the door and take hold of the door handle and swing it gently open. The door swings smoothly on its hinges and you walk into the room, pulling the door shut behind you. As you shut the door, you leave all of your problems, worries, cares and concerns outside. Inside your private room, you are free from these concerns.

You look about you and notice the lighting in the room. It is your own room and decorated to your own liking. You take note of the colours on the walls and furnishings. You survey the range of furniture. Finally, you note the carpet or floor coverings and feel the sensations of the texture under your feet.

You now walk over to the comfortable couch and stretch out, sinking down into the cushions. Almost feeling yourself moving down, ... down, ... down into the cushions. The room is so quiet and so relaxing ... very relaxing. No cares, problems, worries or concerns. Just you. Very peaceful. Very quiet and so ... so ... relaxing.

In practice, you will probably only want to use one of the above focusing techniques, but several have been presented for variety. At this point, it might help if you did some running in place to get yourself back into an alert and receptive state. If you were reading the focusing passages to attain a state of relaxation, then delete the running and enjoy the relaxation state that follows.

Positive self-suggestions

The use of positive self-suggestions is a very important part of maximising your effectiveness at work. When you are relaxed, you will note that your body has slowed down. Your heart rate will be slower, your breathing rate will be slower; in fact most of your bodily functions will be pleasantly slow and easy. Even your mind will be less active, although still aware of what is happening. When your mind is relatively quiet and calm, you can present constructive messages to yourself. While the exact mechanism is unclear, these messages are received and registered by the mind and can act to positively affect your work performance.

It is very important to say here and now that using positive self-messages in the absence of any real background preparation and conscientious application will result in comfortable job stagnation. That is, the practice of relaxing yourself and feeding yourself unrealistically positive sayings is not going to produce a magical result. The procedure is meant as an adjunct to and an enhancement of thorough work preparation and conscientious application.

Some of the suggestions which you may wish to try are listed below:

- I can relax.
- I can control my mind.
- I can succeed in my work.

You will note that the suggestions are all 'I can' type statements; they are fairly general in their scope; and they are concisely stated. It would be a waste of your time to feed in patently unrealistic messages.

The disbelievers amongst you might be furling your brows and scratching your heads, but the system is worth trying, isn't it? What do you have to lose but a little pessimism or cynicism?

Come back slowly

In order to come out of your relaxed state, count slowly from one to five, feeling yourself becoming more alert with each number. At five, slowly open your eyes and then stretch your arms and legs. Do not get straight up on to your feet as you might become light-headed.

Before doing anything else, notice how relaxed you feel. You might feel a sensation of heaviness in your limbs, or perhaps a feeling of dryness in your mouth. Your body might feel lethargic and reluctant to move. Take a minute or so and just enjoy that relaxed and comfortable feeling.

Plan your next relaxation session

While the positive effects of your present relaxation experience are still with you, take time to plan when you will next practise relaxing. Remember, practice is absolutely essential and an organised approach will be necessary to learn the skill. After a few weeks of practice, you will probably find that the effects of the relaxation experience are so positive that you are actually looking forward to your next practice session.

It is important to emphasise that you should be planning to practise on average twice a day for about fifteen minutes each time over a three-to four-month period to make relaxation a part of your daily routine and a permanent skill. After you have fully learned how to relax, you could go for prolonged periods without relaxing (not that this is recommended) and return to the practice with little or no difficulty. Learning how to relax is much like learning any other skill, such as riding a bicycle or typing. Once learned, the skills are never forgotten. They can be reactivated with little effort after long periods. So, a conscientious three-to four-month learning period can be seen justifiably as a lifetime investment.

As a reminder, draw up a chart on which you can record the number of relaxation practice sessions carried out each day. Place the chart on your mirror or dresser top, or somewhere you are likely to look at the beginning and end of each day. In addition to recording simply the number of practice sessions per day, you might also want to record the depth of relaxation attained, perhaps on a scale of five—one for shallow, five for a very deep response. At a glance, then, you can see how your practice is progressing.

In summary, relaxation training is truly a vital skill which, once learned, will provide daily dividends to you at work, at home and in your leisure. Conscientious practice in necessary, but the time involved is minimal and the practice sessions are thoroughly pleasant.

Summary

Learning to relax is a very important work skill. The focus of the relaxation skill is upon your mind—learning how to maintain self-control when the work environment is getting chaotic and stressful. Learning how to relax will take a few months of daily practice, but the end result is well worth the time and effort. This chapter has presented a detailed step-by-step relaxation method which is summarised below:

- Practise your relaxation skills daily
- Learn how to breathe in a relaxing way
- Control the focus of your mind
- Use positive self-suggestions to facilitate your progress
- Be prepared to practise twice daily, even on very busy days, for a learning period of three to four months

8

Keeping fit, beating stress

How frequently are you ...

( ) Famished by lunchtime because of an inadequate break-
      fast?
( ) Bothered by a weight problem?
( ) Out of breath after climbing a set of stairs?
( ) Feeling negative about yourself because you are out of
      condition?
( ) Missing the regular exercise you might previously have
      had?
( ) Unable to get to sleep because your mind is too excited?
( ) Waking sporadically throughout the night?
( ) Giving up your smoking habit yet again?
( ) Feeling that you depend too much upon alcohol to get
      you through the work day?
( ) Taking anxiety or depression medications?
( ) Putting off holidays because you are too busy?
( ) Working at home during evenings and weekends to keep
      up with your work load?

Sounds disastrous, doesn't it? If you have marked many of the
above items as being characteristic of your work life, then the
results could well be disastrous.

Recent studies on fitness and work have shown conclusively that
physical and emotional well-being are directly related to productivity at work, sick leave, staff turnover and net profits for the
firm. A finding of particular interest is that if fifty per cent of the
adult population undertook sufficient regular physical activity to
gain protection against cardiovascular disease, an estimated saving
of $274 million per annum would occur. A United States study
found that employee sickness was costing US business $40 billion

each year. In response to these studies conducted over the last decade, businesses around the world have built gyms and started fitness programs to encourage workers to get fit and stay fit.

These programs benefit employees as well as employers. Healthy employees have fewer minor illnesses and they report experiencing greater satisfaction at their work. They have also been found to have fewer accidents and when an accident is experienced, the fit people recuperate faster than the unfit.

What health benefits can you expect from giving some time to promoting your fitness? Here are some of the results which have been reported:

- Decrease in your blood pressure.
- Reduction or cessation of smoking.
- Reduction in your cardiac risk factors.
- Improved oxygen uptake by your body tissues.
- Improved morale.
- Reduction in body weight.
- Improved diet.
- Reduction in alcohol consumption.
- Less sickness.
- Improved self-image.
- Expansion of friendship circles.

Having hopefully argued a strong and convincing case for health and fitness, how can you manage it? This chapter will present some suggestions on how you, the worker, can actively become more healthy by addressing the following issues: eating a sound diet; exercising; sleeping well; dealing with smoking, drinking and medication problems; and using your leisure time constructively.

Eating a nutritious diet

For most people, eating presents many pleasures but also some problems. Even though eating is a necessity, the basics of good nutrition are often misunderstood and frequently abused. This section will discuss some general issues relating to foods and eating and will present some general guidelines for a healthy diet.

Eating food is for most of us one of our first and also last pleasures in life. While eating is basic to our daily living, many people abuse their eating habits. Ideally, food should be considered to have nutrition value only. Eating should not be looked upon as a reward and food deprivation should not be used as a punishment.

While nutrition and dietetics go beyond the scope of this book, it is important to alert readers to one of the most common eating problems—obesity. Many workers are overweight and a large number of these people seek magical cures from the latest diets. As a general rule, diets alone will not solve most obesity problems. Self-understanding, a well-planned diet and regular exercise will be necessary to deal with entrenched problems of obesity. Getting fit is not easy, but help can be obtained from a psychologist or from your family doctor.

James consulted me about recurring depressions, but his physical appearance and the history of his problem revealed that obesity was one of the central features requiring attention. He had been a retail pharmacist for sixteen years and had become frustrated with his job. In addition to working on various aspects of his work problems, I suggested a behaviour control program to assist him in losing weight. Essentially, the program restricted or deleted situations where he snacked at food. Guidelines were also established about his eating at meal times. A daily exercise program was set and he attended weekly meetings with me during which his weight was recorded. After ten weeks on the program, he had lost twenty one pounds and was noticeably looking better. The positive remarks he received from friends and clients strongly encouraged his progress. After many previous attempts at dieting, he now feels optimistic about his weight reduction.

The following guidelines were part of the program established for James and might be helpful to you in planning how to maintain a more healthy diet and lifestyle.

Dietary guidelines:

- Focus upon getting fit and healthy rather than just losing weight.
- Plan for both exercising and healthy eating. Get professional advice about the most beneficial exercise possibilities for you.
- Enlist the support of others living or working with you— changing your eating and exercising habits can cause some personal inconvenience and some mild discomfort. The

battle will be more easily fought with good support and encouragement.

- Consult a dietitian or a state government nutritionist for advice about healthy foods and healthy eating.
- Avoid snacking. If you must nibble, try celery or carrot sticks.
- Limit your eating to one place, generally the kitchen or dining room table.
- Eat slowly and savour each mouthful.
- Be aware of eating when bored. Keep your mind actively occupied by pursuing a new interest.
- Limit your sugar intake, both obvious (on cereal, or in drinks) and hidden (in cakes, biscuits, etc.).
- Substitute complex carbohydrates (fruits, vegetables) for refined sugar. The complex carbohydrates will supply energy for longer periods and they contain other nutrients as well.
- Don't keep sweets, chocolates, cakes, cookies and other problem foods around the house or workplace. Put temptation at a distance; the longer the distance, the better.
- If you miss the crunch of crispy snack foods, try banana chips or sunflower seeds.
- Decrease your salt consumption. It's a cardiovascular stressor.
- Monitor your alcohol consumption. A standard drink of beer (200 mls) or a glass of wine has 500 kilojoules and no other nutrients. Alternate sips of wine with sips of water.
- Place a food consumption chart on the fridge door and record what you eat.
- Use small plates and keep the serving dishes off the table so as to minimise the temptation to have additional servings.
- Don't shop when you are hungry. Restrict your food purchases to the items on your shopping list.
- Chart your daily weight each morning to monitor how your eating and exercising plan is progressing. Don't expect instant results from a new diet/exercise program. Be satisfied with a regular loss of about one-half to one kilogram a week.

- Limit your caffeine intake to 500 mg per day, the limit of your liver in detoxifying the caffeine. (One average strength cup of coffee contains 100 mg of caffeine; tea, 65 mg.)

While these are general guidelines, you may wish to structure your approach to a healthy diet on more specific suggestions. Try the dietary suggestions in the worker's diet below.

A sample worker's diet

Breakfast
  Plain cereal, left-over boiled rice or boiled wheat with just a sprinkle of sugar. If you choose other cereals, check the salt and sugar content on the package. Wholemeal toast or bread, but delete margarine, butter and jam. Fruit juice or a piece of fruit.
  Tea or coffee, preferably black.
Lunch
  Wholemeal bread sandwich with any protein-rich filling (e.g., cheese, egg, cold meat).
  Salad with lots of green vegetables.
  Piece of fresh fruit.
  Tea or coffee, preferably black.
Dinner
  Choose a lean meat from fish, veal, chicken or have a vegetarian main course.
  Whatever your main course, serve with appropriate vegetables (steamed) and potato, rice or pasta.
  Dessert, if necessary, can be rice pudding or a cheese platter.
  Tea or coffee.

While the diet suggests certain foods as being desirable, there are also some foods which should be monitored carefully and consumed the least: sugar, oil, butter and margarine; foods eaten in moderation should include milk, cheese, yoghurt, lean meat, poultry, fish, legumes, nuts and eggs; and foods which should be eaten in preference include cereals, bread, vegetables and fruits.

It is important to emphasise that the diet outlined above is a general guideline. To make it work for you, it will be necessary to incorporate variety and some creativity to render the foods appealing and satisfying. Once again, consult an experienced dietitian for further advice about modifying your diet to accomodate a healthier lifestyle.

In summary, the working person's diet is very important. The foods eaten in the morning, at noon and at night can affect the quantity and quality of one's work. Eating wisely can make you a happier person and a more productive worker.

Exercising regularly

The role of exercise has already been mentioned in the preceding section. Quite apart from contributing to weight loss, exercising on a regular basis can keep you physically fit and emotionally sound. But where do you start and how do go about regaining and maintaining a physically fit body?

Many people who participated in sport during their school years will recall the pain and agony sessions on the training fields, in the pool or at other sport venues. Yes, they were exhausting, but often exhilarating sessions. But, having prospered from these training experiences years ago, should you go back to the same regimen to get fit again? Decidedly not! The former athlete who tries to step briskly and vehemently into the old training program risks injury to the muscles and bones and possibly even a heart attack or stroke.

If you have not had a background in sport or regular exercise and you are decidedly plump, you may feel some embarrass-ment at the thought of going to a gym where everyone appears to be fit and trim. Speak with a person at the gym about your embarrassment. There could be special getting started classes or groups which cater to your special needs and sensitivities. The important point to keep prominently in mind is that getting fit is a positive step forward to a more healthy future.

How should you get started on your fitness campaign?

Step 1   Start carefully and slowly

See your doctor and have yourself checked for participation in a fitness program. You might wish to consult a fitness specialist at a reputable gym or at a nearby university. Essentially, you want to find an exercise program which is: (1) enjoyable; (2) convenient; and (3) suitable for your age and state of fitness. The essence of an exercise program is to use the large muscles of the body in a repetitive fashion such that you increase you pulse rate to 70–85 per cent of its maximum level. You can calculate your exercising heart rate by subtracting your age from 220, the average maximum heart rate, and multiplying this figure by 0.75. For example, a 40-year-old person would ideally exercise at or about the following value: $220 - 40 = 180 \times 0.75 = 135$ beats per minute. In order to measure your state of exertion, simply take your pulse for ten seconds and multiply by six. A healthy 40-year-old male should try to maintain a pulse rate of between 125–145 beats per minute over a 20–30 minute period three to five times a week for maximum effectiveness. For sedentary workers who have not exercised for years, you are advised to work up to this level over a time period recommended by your doctor or exercise consultant.

Step 2 *Choose your exercise*

You may find brisk walking, jogging, cycling, or swimming appealing. They are all beneficial types of exercise. Other options include skating, skipping rope, rowing, orienteering, or exercising to music. You need not exercise every day, for studies have shown that the body needs time to rest and repair. As stated above, exercising three to five times a week is ideal. There were fewer injuries and accidents recorded in groups of people exercising at this rate.

Step 3 *Maintain the program*

Busy people can quickly dismiss their scheduled exercise when the pace at their work quickens. It is important to recognise that your exercise sessions will enhance your work performance and give you a necessary and beneficial break from the grind. We can easily take our health for granted—until sickness intervenes. One way of getting your exercise automatically is to cycle or walk to work. This option will not be possible for everyone, but those who live reasonably close to their work can commute and exercise at the same time. Other exercise suggestions include:

- Never take elevators or escalators when you can climb the stairs.
- Consider parking your car several blocks away from your destination and walking the remaining distance.
- Do some workplace exercises frequently throughout your work day such as stretching your arms and legs, bending your upper body and twisting your torso.
- While standing and waiting, do some isometric exercises like clasping your hands and pressing your arms towards each other. Pressing your lower leg against a wall can have the same effect upon your leg muscles.

- Sedentary workers, especially those using typewriters, word processors and computers, should enquire about exercises which will warm them up for their workday and prevent problems such as repetitive strain injuries. Contact your state health department for advice.

A few words of warning are relevant at this point. Exercise can be taken to extremes and become harmful, even addictive. If you find that: you are ignoring your work responsibilities or your family in order to exercise; or you are reacting with irritability when you miss a day of exercise; or you are going out to exercise in extreme weather conditions which could be potentially dangerous—then perhaps you are taking your exercising to extremes.

In summary exercising regularly each week is important to your physical health and your work performance. See your doctor before starting fitness training and consult an exercise specialist about a suitable program. If discipline is not your strong suit, then pair up with a colleague and get fit together. You are much more likely to make that extra effort to get started and keep going if you are working out with a friend.

Sleeping soundly

Following on from relaxation, diet and exercise, a fourth fitness factor important to the working person is sleep. There is still a gap in our scientific understanding about what sleep actually does for us. Probably the most popular theory is that sleep recharges our batteries.

While the physiological reason for sleep remains obscure, we do know that there are two types of sleep: rapid eye movement (REM) sleep and non-rapid eye movement (NREM) sleep. In the first few hours of sleep, the eyes remain still (NREM), but then become active. The REM sleep periods are lighter sleep states and the times during which dreaming occurs. We have several REM sleep periods alternating with the NREM periods and it is perfectly possible to have several dreams in one night.

Many people worry about the amount of sleep they are getting. Some think they are sleeping too much and others worry they are not sleeping enough. The vital question which most ask is: How much sleep do I need? The answer depends upon the individual.

Some people are comfortable and work well during the day with as little as three or four hours of sleep at night. Others may feel they require as much as twelve or thirteen hours for effective daytime functioning.

Recent sleep research has found that the average sleep period is seven and three-quarters hours.

In spite of the above facts, many people may persist in believing they have a sleep problem. Sleep experts suggest that a person has a sleep problem only if the inability to sleep interferes with daytime functioning, no matter how many hours are spent asleep. Thus, if you sleep for relatively few hours most nights and spend some of the potential sleep time tossing and turning, but still function well most days, then you probably don't have a sleep problem. However, if you do have a sleep problem, try the relaxation approach described in Chapter 7 or see your doctor.

Smoking, drinking and medications

These three health problems are major issues and a definitive discussion goes well beyond the scope of this book. However, it is important to deal at least briefly with each one.

The health consequences of tobacco smoking have been well-publicised and documented. The evidence is conclusive—tobacco smoking is related to lung cancer, cardiovascular disease, and pulmonary problems, to mention but a few health difficulties. While it is each individual's right to decide whether or not to smoke, it is not fair to affect those around you. Increasingly, 'no smoking' zones are being established in public places. Many offices are now restricting smoking to areas which are not going to affect non-smokers. If you work in an area where smoking is presently permitted and you are concerned or annoyed by the smoke, discuss the problem with your boss.

Alcoholism and regular drinking excesses are also major problems for many people, both at work and at home. Drinking on the job is not generally condoned and, if discovered, often warrants a stern reprimand from the management. However, reprimands can be ineffectual if there is a deeply-entrenched drinking problem. If you depend upon alcohol to get you started at the beginning of the day and are sneaking drinks during the day, you have a serious drinking problem which needs attention. The first step towards recovery is admitting that there is a problem. Once the problem is admitted, then outside help should be sought. Your family doctor or Alcoholics Anonymous are good sources of assistance.

Just as alcohol dependency can undermine your work effectiveness, there are many drugs which people take in a dependent way. Some of the most commonly abused medications are the minor tranquilisers (Valium and similar drugs), headache pills, and sleep medications. If you have been taking medications for extended periods, discuss the issue with your doctor. There could be alternatives to medication which can be explored.

Benefiting from leisure time

Most readers will be familiar with the adage, All work and no play makes Jack/Jill a dull person. Many major business firms are now taking that saying to heart, by encouraging their employees to become involved in hobbies and other interest activities outside of work time.

'But what can a hobby do about a real work problem?' you might justifiably ask. The hobby itself is not going to solve a problem, but it can provide a positive distraction. As well as distracting you, the hobby or interest could well extend you academically, socially or psychologically.

Almost any type of interest or hobby will do. The essential quality should be enjoyment. Ideally, you should have a basic interest in the activity and a desire to work at it. However, it is important that your chosen leisure activity does not become a problem. For example, I recall vividly a very dynamic and aggressive businessman who was at his office at 7.15 a.m. every weekday (and some weekends as well). He faced a continual onslaught of problems and decisions which caused a major stress problem. His doctor suggested that he return to tennis, a game he had played at school. However, his tennis games were characterised by the same ruthless, almost savage competetiveness that was creating his stress problem at work. If stress is a problem, then look for low-stress or no-stress leisure activities.

One final word about leisure and work—do not put off taking your holidays. Getting away from work periodically can make you a happier person and a better and more productive worker on your return. Plan a variety of activities for your holidays and, of course, discuss your wishes with other members of the family if you live in a family situation.

Summary

This chapter has presented several approaches to a healthier, happier and more productive work life. Being healthy at work contributes to a more satisfying and more productive work experience. The following issues were discussed:

- Maintaining a nutritionally sound diet
- Participating in a regular exercise program
- Sleeping well
- Decreasing smoking, drinking and non-essential medications
- Pursuing hobbies and interests outside of work
- Taking your holidays regularly

9

Sharpening communication skills

During your workdays, do you ...

( ) Try to see and hear yourself from the other person's vantage point?

( ) Regret having said certain things to others without thinking first?

( ) Extend yourself to be interested and enthused in your dealings with others?

( ) Dress appropriately for your work tasks and commitments?

( ) Listen carefully with your eyes and ears when talking with others?

( ) Get uncontrollably nervous when expected to speak in a group conversation or at a meeting?

Some of the items noted above might be familiar to you or characteristic of a colleague. Communication skills at the workplace are very important. Even with a high level of job-related technical skills, the employee who is deficient in appropriate communication skills will be certainly disadvantaged.

Depending on the type of work you do, communicating can occupy up to 80 per cent or more of the average working day and that's a lot of time to be wasted if your communication skills are not finely tuned and working well.

Communicating is far from just a verbal process. In fact, you cannot *not* communicate. Essentially, just your presence or even your absence from the workplace communicates. The words you choose, the way you hold your body, the clothes you wear and even the way you sit and walk can communicate messages about you. It is not the intention here to make you overly sensitised and critical about your communication potential. It is very important, though, to make you aware of both your verbal communication skills and your body language. How you manage these communication channels will determine, to a large extent, your work success.

This chapter will present several basic guidelines on how to communicate more effectively at work, including: verbal and non-verbal skills; listening skills; and the use of courtesy and tactfulness. The chapter will conclude with a brief discussion of two important communication problems, shyness at the workplace and public speaking anxiety.

Communicating verbally

Verbal communication is the process of transmitting messages by words or sounds. To communicate verbally, we ideally select the most effective words for the occasion and then present them in a fluent and understandable way.

Selecting the most effective words can be critical. An important, but often underrated duty for the worker is to learn the basic vocabulary of the job. You will want to note particularly the names of people who can assist you with various aspects of your work; the names of the various sections, departments or work units at the organisation; and the names of procedures and processes which are important to your job.

Perhaps the following case can illustrate the importance of maintaining an up-to-date knowledge of the technical language of the workplace. George, a bank accountant, recently sought counselling on the recommendation of his doctor because of severe stress reactions to his work. He was 54 years old and had been with the bank for 28 years. In the early years of his career, he found the work to be stimulating and challenging, but over the past ten years, he had become increasingly dissatisfied. His most recent review had mentioned poor report writing and some difficulties getting along well with the junior staff. During the interview, George mentioned that he felt threatened by the recent computerisation of the banking industry. He did not understand much of the new computer terminology and reacted negatively to the younger staff who communicated in this new and incomprehensible language. One of the recommendations I made to George was that he enrol in a course, 'Communicating with Computers,' sponsored by a corporate education firm. After completing the course, George felt more at ease and far less threatened at work. His new communication skills, coupled with other stress management procedures, allowed George to progress more happily and competently with his job.

No matter what your work position, it is critical that you develop a working knowledge of the key terms and concepts used frequently at your workplace. If you are new on the job, keep a notebook in a handy pocket and when you hear a new term which seems to be important, write it down and ask then or later what the term means. The key to building your vocabulary is to use the new terms frequently. There is little benefit in simply collecting the terms in a notebook. At the beginning of each day, pick several terms or concepts which you have not used since noting them and make a point of using them appropriately some time that day.

Just as important as the words and terms you use, is how you use them. One of the best and most convenient ways of improving your verbal communication skills is simply to listen very carefully to good communicators. We live in a social laboratory. Observe those around you and then experiment with the new skills.

Your observations will no doubt quickly demonstrate wide variations in communication styles. Effective verbal communication goes far beyond just selecting the most appropriate words. Good communicators adapt their speech volume, pace and style to the occasion. They also vary their vocal inflections to produce emphasis or special mood effects; and, very importantly, they enunciate clearly. To get all of these verbal skills working together, and well, can be difficult and practice will certainly be necessary to produce a good result.

I have a friend who is bright and witty, but regrettably much of what he says is lost to me and others because he speaks far too quickly. Other people tend to mumble, speak too softly or drone on in a boring monotone. If you suspect that your speaking skills need some polishing, tape record a conversation with a friend and then replay it. Ask your friend to offer constructive criticism on how you can improve your speaking skills.

Prior to important meetings, try rehearsing what you want to say. Based upon what you know of the other person(s), plan your approach and words and then practise them—but do not depend upon parrot-like presentations of set lines. If time permits, tape or video record your practice session and polish your skills following the replays. As I suggested, communicating effectively is a very complex process. If you have difficulty mastering all of the various components, then consider seeking assistance from a communication skills trainer. Your firm may have a training officer or the personnel department may be able to recommend an appropriate person. Learning how to communicate well certainly warrants your prompt attention.

As mentioned earlier in this book, effective workers are sensitive to the needs of the organisation and to the people with whom they work. They observe, listen, think and then react effectively to their colleagues, customers and others at the workplace. Their verbal skills vary from casual chitchat over lunch to delicate interchanges such as handling a customer's complaint or dealing with an angry colleague. The skills are complex but perfectly within grasp of the worker who wishes to progress. Whether you practise on your own or with others, practice is the hallmark of progress.

The essence, then, of effective verbal communication is to observe, listen and then think before you speak. The short pause during which you plan and prepare your thoughts will help you to express yourself more clearly and concisely.

Communicating non-verbally

Non-verbal communication, or body language, as it has been called in the popular press, is the way we communicate bodily. While entire books have been written on this fascinating topic, only a brief overview will be possible here. Interested readers should consult the reference list at the back of this book for additional sources.

Non-verbal communication can be divided for present purposes into various types: eye contact; facial expression; body movements, including gesturing and posturing; and non-body communications such as clothing.

Eye contact

Eye contact is a very important adjunct to effective interpersonal communication. The familiar expressions, 'shifty eyes' and 'bedroom eyes' are but two popular examples of eye-based communication. Given that our eye behaviour is so important, what should we do with our eyes in order to create the most positive impression? Here are a few suggestions.

- Try to maintain comfortable eye contact with your conversation partner. In casual interactions, you might find maintaining eye contact between 50 and 70 per cent of the time to be comfortable and productive.
- When walking, keep your head up and look at others as you pass. These brief eye contacts give recognition to the other people and may promote more involvement at a future time.
- Looking away from a speaker, or fixing your gaze skyward or at the ground will probably cause the speaker to think you are either disinterested, rude, or lacking in confidence.
- When it is important to establish trust in a relationship, refrain from wearing sunglasses so that the other person can see your eyes.
- For those who wear contact lenses, air conditioned offices can dry the surface of the lens and cause frequent blinking, creating the impression of a nervous tick. Consult your optometrist if you are bothered by this problem.

Facial expressions

The face contains a very complex and intricate set of muscles enabling it to exhibit a wide range of different expressions. Researchers have extensively studied facial expressions and their findings fill entire volumes. Only a few expressions will be discussed here: smiling, scowling/frowning, and stern/serious.

Smiling has been said to be a reciprocal expression in that those who smile frequently get smiled at frequently. It's no secret that a smile tends to warm a relationship. At the workplace, starting the day with a smile and a few words of greeting to those around you can create a positive feeling both in you and your workmates. Smiling can also make an introduction more than just a formality. And, when things get tense and tight as in a confrontation, a smile used at just the right time can help smooth rough waters and facilitate a resolution. If your smile has been in cold storage, get it out and warm it up. Stand in front of the bathroom mirror and smile, smile, smile. Your cheek muscles might hurt because they are out of condition, but systematic practice will help.

Scowling, or furling the eyebrows to create a gloomy or

malevolent expression, can be the external sign of stress and strain. Ben, a former client, was continually dissatisfied at work and jumped from job to job. One of the features which characterised his appearance was his constant scowl. The scowling continued until he realised how negatively he looked. He worked hard at softening his expression and when he smiled more often, he found that others showed more interest in him. With his scowl reduced, he was more frequently invited into group discussions and other activities at work. People such as Ben may be unaware of the effect which their facial expressions have upon others. It is fair to say that few of us would want to look continually gloomy and foreboding. What can be done? Once again, bathroom mirror practice can help. Another approach is to practise recounting anecdotes and possibly trying a few safe jokes. Hopefully, they will be successful and others will laugh. If they don't, you should. Being able to laugh at yourself is an important aspect of positive interpersonal behaviour. And, it is quite difficult to be laughing and scowling at the same time.

Stern and serious expressions abound in tense environments. When the pressure is high, faces get stern. Your facial expression is often a reflection of what is happening emotionally within you. When the pressure is high and you are thinking, 'My God, what if I can't make that deadline?' your facial expression will hardly be showing a toothy grin. There are certainly tense times in any workplace, but looking for the lighter side can help you and your workmates. Part of the secret of breaking through seriousness is to be more relaxed. Learning how to control your mind and worry less is a certain step forward. You might want to go back over Chapter 7 on relaxation in case you haven't already started on a training program.

Body movements

People from some cultures make very ample use of their hands, arms and torso when they speak. Perhaps they take to heart the adage that a picture, even if it is an animated body picture, is worth a thousand words. With some people, you will find both animated body language and a thousand words! No matter whether you are at work or leisure, supplementing your spoken words with appropriate gestures and postural motions will generally enhance your communication. Watch others who are animated communicators and note how and when they use their bodies to supplement what they say. If you have been static and reserved in the use of your body, try to loosen up. Here are some pointers on how to make your body language speak more effectively.

- Keep your hands in front of you at about waist height so that they are ready to go into motion. Don't immobilise them by holding them behind your back or clasped in front.

- Practise using finger and hand signals which are compatible with your words. Watch the gestures used by good communicators and try to put similar movements into your conversations when appropriate.

- Monitor the foot movements of others when they are sitting. Foot movements are the least controlled part of the body and you can make interesting inferences about the internal state of others by observing what their feet are doing.

- In order to facilitate gestural and postural movements, stand rather than sit. Your body has much more freedom when not constrained by a chair.

- In your leisure time, consider playing charades or other party games which require you to act out various themes without speaking. Loosen your inhibitions and get your body into action.

- If reading about body language and observing others fails to improve your non-verbal communication, join an acting class. The classes should certainly help you to loosen your body and make it more expressive.

Clothing

What shall I wear today? would probably be one of your earliest daily thoughts. The question is easily answered if you wear a work uniform. However, if you don't, choosing your clothes can be an important decision. Why? Because to some extent what we wear is a message about ourselves—a communication.

As a communication exercise, sit near a busy intersection some lunchtime and observe the passers-by. Focus upon certain people and try to guess what sort of person the individual is by the clothes being worn. Is the person wearing the latest fashions or more conservative clothes? Are the colours vibrant or muted? Are there any accessories? After these practice sessions, test your observational skill by trying to guess the inner qualities of the people you meet at a party. Check your inferences later in a conversation with the host or hostess.

In order to promote more communication via your clothes, consider wearing some small but conversation-provoking item. For men, an unusual necktie will often do the job. My father collected outrageous neckties and wore them to work, parties and other events. They were true conversation pieces. One tie which I inherited has a repeated motif of St. Bernard dogs with the letters DETYS inscribed under each dog. The motif is large and almost always draws questions about the meaning. By the way, the meaning of the letters is Don't Eat The Yellow Snow.

Having mentioned the possibility of using clothes as a message medium, it is important to add that this communication channel can be overdone. If you are in doubt about the suitability of your clothes, ask for advice from a friend or two. But, do take the bold step and try some interesting clothing ideas. Start with small steps and be prepared to take these risks in order to enhance both your communication ability and your confidence.

Listening

Listening is a skill which is often slighted, or ignored altogether. Why do people listen poorly? Good question! Perhaps it's because we take the skill for granted. Or, maybe it's because, 'Listen!' has been presented *ad nauseum* as a command by fierce and frustrated teachers and parents, thus casting the activity in a negative light. Whatever the reason, effective listening is a skill which is commonly in short supply but a most valuable asset when learned and practised.

The complexity of the listening process is best understood from the Chinese symbol for the word listen. The symbol represented below is comprised of the integral parts of effective listening: the ear, you, eyes, undivided attention and the heart. I believe that sums up the listening process admirably. To listen well is, indeed, a mixture of hearing, seeing, attending and empathising. Missing one or more parts of the process means possibly missed information.

EAR · YOU · EYES · UNDIVIDED ATTENTION · HEART

Your workplace listening skills can be important in many different ways. For example, listening and understanding your initial instructions about how to do your job is critical. Good listeners work actively at the listening process. Their eyes and ears are attending and receiving information and their minds are working at understanding what is being communicated. Questions such as, Is this important? If so, how? should be continually considered during important meetings and conferences. Workplace messages could be straightforward instructions, or they could be more complicated types of communication, such as an obtuse interaction between several people. No matter what the content, if you want to communicate well, you must master the listening process. Here are a few pointers about how to listen better.

- When it is important to listen closely, work actively at the process. Clear other matters from your mind so that you can give the speaker your full and undivided attention.

- Observe carefully the signs and signals of the speaker. Note carefully the speaker's body language—eye movements; facial expressions; gestures; and postural shifts.

- If there is background noise or other distractions, suggest that you move to a more suitable location.

- If you don't have sufficient time to complete the discussion, arrange a time and place for a further meeting. Feeling rushed can be a significant distractor to effective listening.

- In order to ensure that you have understood what has been said, periodically summarise the essence of the discussion.
- When confusion occurs during the interaction, clarify the matter as soon as possible so that further listening is not compromised.
- When listening to complicated discussions, consider making notes in a notebook to ensure that you get the critical details.
- At the end of an important meeting, mentally summarise the important points. If you think you might confuse some of the points, jot them down in a notebook.

Courtesy and tact

Courtesy and tact are communication skills which are other-or-oriented. That is, your words and behaviour are geared around the feelings and sensitivities of those with whom you are speaking.

Take for example answering the telephone. We all are familiar with the alienating feeling when a telephonist blurts out, 'Jones & Smith' when answering the company's telephone. The mellifluous responses, 'Good morning, Jones & Smith', and 'One moment please' are all too frequently omitted. Pleasantly voiced 'please' and 'thankyou' take virtually no time, cost nothing to the company or telephonist, but can create a warm and welcoming feeling to the caller. Given that first impressions are very important, courtesy and tactfulness on the telephone and at the reception desk are critical.

The basic principle in enhancing courtesy and tactfulness is to think, If I were the other person, how would I feel if this were said to me? In essence, you put yourself in the other person's position and test your feelings.

Another communication situation, which can often be upsetting, is handling a confrontation. Too often in these interchanges, personal emotions fly forwards and backwards and nothing constructive is accomplished. Even though confrontations can be quite complex interactions, there are several steps which can help to resolve the situation constructively. Step one: keep as calm and composed as possible. Step two: take into account the feelings of the other person. Look at the predicament from the other person's perspective. Step three: carefully choose your words and your approach (be tactful) so that the other person's feelings are not threatened. Step four: try to find a solution to the immediate situation which will accommodate both parties' needs for the time being. Arrange a subsequent meeting to discuss the issue at greater length.

Why should I be courteous and tactful? you might ask. Chiefly because these communication qualities can make you feel better about your relationships with your workmates. Courtesy and tact at the workplace mean that your work can progress more smoothly and productively. These positive communication skills can also open up new job possibilities for you. Glance through the employment ads and you will find 'must be a good communicator' quoted frequently in the requirements for many positions. Courtesy and tact are generally not specified, but they would certainly be esteemed qualities in the minds of most employers. If you want further information about these critical communication skills, ask the librarian at your local library for books on communication skills, etiquette, and interpersonal relationships.

Communication problems

While communication problems can abound in any workplace, there are two specific problems which I wish to address here: shyness at work and public speaking anxiety. Both problems are surprisingly common and can be veritable anchors on the heels of capable employees who wish to progress in their work.

Shyness at work

Shyness affects just about everyone under certain situations. While most people cope reasonably well with occasional shyness, there are some who live in a personal prison, unable to reach out and make friends or relate positively to others. Being shy at work can severely limit work effectiveness, unless of course, you work generally on your own with little or no contact with others.

Shy people present themselves at work in many varied ways. There is the quiet wallflower who fades into the background and is not often noticed. At the opposite extreme, there is the raging extrovert who can be loud, aggressive and abrasive, but who finds it difficult to relate on an intimate level to others. In between, there are many other people, such as the knocker, the person who knocks or degrades others.

Given the complex presenting pictures of the shy person, what can be done about the problem? Firstly, the shy person must admit that a problem exists. It could be anxiety about attending and participating in meetings or contributing to the small talk over the lunch table. No matter how the shyness presents, if you are shy at work, admit there is a problem and then do something about it.

Having resolved to do something about your shyness, ask yourself to what extent the following aspects contribute to the overall problem— severe nervousness when relating to others; uncertainty about what to say or how to communicate generally; lack of self confidence. Research has shown that these three aspects are the central issues in most shyness problems. Let's look briefly at each and see what might be done to help.

If you feel nervous about dealing with others at work, learn how to relax yourself. Turn to Chapter 7 and be prepared to spend 15 to 30 minutes each day practising the relaxation exercises. When you have learned how to relax, get relaxed and imagine yourself dealing comfortably with typical communication situations at work. By systematically linking the feeling of relaxation with these imagined scenes, you will learn how to communicate in a more comfortable and competent way. Should you experience difficulties with the technique, consult a psychologist for assistance.

While learning how to relax is reasonably straightforward, learning how to make friends, maintain relationships and handle the many ups and downs of people is a much more daunting task. Consult the reading list at the end of this book or ask your local librarian for advice. You might also find some helpful reading material by browsing the shelves of a good bookshop. Following your reading, you will benefit most from trying out the various skills. This can be a bit frightening, but ask yourself what is the worst possible outcome of trying a new skill. Generally, the worst outcome is just transient embarrassment. So, have a go each day, speaking with new people, asking questions, entering into progressively more lengthy conversations and generally building your communication skill repertoire. Once again, if you have difficulty, a psychologist specialising in communication skills will be able to help.

Low self-confidence, the last of the three aspects of shyness, is the most challenging. In many ways, your confidence will increase as you discover how to control those panicky feelings and how to perform comfortably and competently with others. However, if your confidence has been only ankle high and your expectations are sky high, some additional help may be needed to provide a boost to get you started.

I recently counselled a young man, David, who was in his first year of employment. He had been shy most of his life and instead of confronting his interpersonal difficulties, he applied himself to his studies. Academically speaking, he was on top of the mountain and was able to get a good job with an international mining company. However, once in the job, he was expected to communicate effectively with others as well as deal with his particular responsibilities. Here are some of the pointers I gave David to help him climb out of his difficulty.

- List your major achievements and skills. If you have achieved in the past, you can do it again.
- Think about your long-terms goals and ask yourself what you can do today to work towards those goals.
- Set a daily goal each day to compliment someone at work.
- Smile appropriately at others when speaking with them.
- Practise looking confident and others will treat you as a confident person.

In summary, shyness can only be overcome by actively working on the integral parts of the problem. Speak with someone new and participate in the lunchtime small talk each day. Be informed about current events, entertainment, sport and other issues which crop up in daily conversations so that you are prepared to speak when the opportunity arises. By taking an active step each day, you can reach the destination of being far less shy and far more comfortable within yourself and with others.

Public speaking anxiety

Most people cringe at the thought of giving a speech or chairing a meeting. The limelight is on you and everyone is watching and listening. Who wouldn't feel at least a bit on edge under these circumstances? While many can muster their courage to get through these events, there are some who find their limbs shaking and their foreheads perspiring at the very thought of the next public speaking occasion.

The prevalence of the problem has led to the formation of public speaking clubs such as Toastmasters, Toastmistresses and Rostrum. These groups exist to help their members gain confidence and skill when presenting a talk, chairing a meeting or being in the limelight for other reasons. Your personnel manager, doctor or other helping professional will be able to suggest the nearest source of help.

If, perchance, there is not a public speaking club in your locale or if you choose to address the problem on your own, then turn to Chapter 7 and get started on the relaxation training procedure. When you have mastered the art of relaxing, then get relaxed and imagine yourself in front of the group to which you will be speaking. Make the scene as realistic as possible by noting the sights, sounds, the tactile stimuli (the feel of the lectern, desk or table in front of you), and perhaps even the smell of the room. If you experience any anxiety or nervousness, say Stop! to yourself and then get relaxed again. Repeat the process until you can stay calm and composed during the entire scene.

Sharon, a young university lecturer, was feeling anxious prior to every lecture and tutorial meeting. Her major worry was that the sheets of notes she had prepared would shake and rattle if she picked them up in front of the class. Consequently, she memorised the entire set of notes prior to her classes. Rather than avoid confronting the problem any longer, she sought help. We worked through the relaxation exercises but also dealt with topics such as humour. She had never prepared anecdotes, humourous stories or jokes as part of her lecture preparation. In fact, she initially baulked at the suggestion that humour has a part in a good lecture. However, she gathered some amusing stories and jokes and practised telling them to me several times. Her confidence increased and she was quite frankly amazed at the very positive response she received in the next lecture. The students were bright-eyed and alert instead of half asleep. She now jots down good stories when she hears them and files them in a humour box. Apart from gathering good jokes, Sharon profited from the opportunity to practise her presentation and receive feedback in a safe, constructive environment. Perhaps you can arrange a similar opportunity if you are feeling shaky when asked to speak in front of others.

Summary

Being an effective communicator is an important personal and workplace skill. Employers prefer good communicators because they listen intently and can work agreeably with colleagues to get the job done quickly and well. Sharpening your communication skills will require you to focus upon the following:

- Verbal skills
  Knowing the workplace vocabulary
  Speaking clearly and coherently
- Non-verbal skills
  Effective eye contact
  Facial expressions
  Body movements
  Clothing
- Listening skills
- Courtesy and tact
- How to deal with the problems of shyness at work and public speaking anxiety.

10

Dealing with problem people

With reference to a particular person X at work, do you frequently . . .

- Wake up in the morning and immediately think 'Oh no, I've got to face X again today'?
- Store anger throughout the day about X?
- Find yourself frequently in conflict with X?
- Experience jealousy about others' ability to get on with X?
- Back away from confrontations with X and then get angry at yourself because of your inability to act appropriately?
- Disagree or have arguments with your boss, who unfortunately is X?

The person, X, referred to above could be your boss, a workmate, a regular customer or even a visitor to your workplace. Whoever X is, if you are storing up strong negative emotions about this person, then your worklife could well be in torment.

Research studies have found that in any work team of ten or more people, there is a high probability that there will be at least one problem person. A problem person can be defined for present purposes as an individual who consistently causes upset and possible dissension amongst the group. The causes of the distress can often be trivial, but the emotional effects upon the other group members can be significant.

The presence of a problem person in a work group has been found to create increased absenteeism, decreased motivation in the work team, decreased productivity and increased staff turnover. If the problem person is the boss of the work team, these negative effects are considerably increased.

This chapter addresses the issue of how to deal with the problem person at work. As people are complex and their relationships even more complicated, a brief mini-psychology about personalities and their effect at the workplace will be presented first. Following this, several approaches to working with a problem person will be discussed, including: practical confrontation skills; resolving workplace problems; and increasing your own likeability (in case you are a problem person).

Workplace personalities

A leading psychological theorist, H. J. Eysenck, proposed that personality is based upon heredity and can be presented as two dimensions: 1, Extroversion—Introversion; and 2, Neurosis (or Emotionalism)—Stability. These two dimensions can be represented as follows:

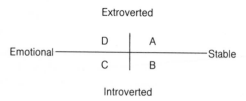

The two intersecting dimensions form four quadrants. Let's look at each of the four quadrants and see what types of personalities are represented.

A   Stable extrovert

These people tend to be outgoing, carefree and assertive individuals who might manifest an unusual trust that everything will work out alright. They socialise readily and carry an aura of casualness about the workings of the firm. This apparent optimistic and carefree approach can be misinterpreted by others as being a lack of genuine commitment and concern for the welfare of the group or firm. The stable extrovert is often a risk-taker and can make a valuable contribution to the organisation in the form of new ideas, new approaches.

B   Stable introvert

The stable introvert can be seen as a loner, a person who thrives on the challenge and stimulation of the job. They are often persistent, conscientious and technically minded. They may prefer to work in research and development situations where there is little interference from others and minimum bother with socialising concerns. They can appear to lack communication skills, but may just prefer to avoid others.

C Emotional introvert

The emotional introvert is a shy and reserved person who avoids risks and favours conformity in the work setting. Job security is a major concern for these people and they tend to enter the organisation, persist and retire, often with little movement to other jobs outside the firm. While they can be self-sufficient, they do tend to doubt their own abilities, thus avoiding any risk taking activity.

D Emotional extrovert

The emotional extrovert is a highly energetic person who is often seen as being aggressive and impulsive. While these people can be irritating, especially when stress is high, their exuberance and impulsiveness can shake sleepy workplaces into new directions. The emotional extrovert can be very temperamental and given to explosive outbursts. Their instability and proneness to excesses can be balanced by their ability to innovate.

You might have identified various people with whom you work from the brief synopses above. Hopefully, not all of these people will be problem people for you. As problem people can cause much tension and turmoil at work, what can you do about these people and the psychological distress which they generate?

Before describing the interpersonal strategies which might be used, it is important to say that problem people are major sources of stress at work. If you are stressed daily from encounters with a problem person, it is imperative that you look after your physical and emotional fitness very carefully. Be certain to eat well, sleep well, and get a good physical workout (just 30 minutes of brisk walking will do) three to five times per week. Being healthy and fit and feeling positive and confident about yourself will make the stress of the problem person less traumatic. Now, let's turn to some interpersonal strategies which might help you sort out the difficulty with the problem person.

Practical confrontation skills

Being able to stand up to people and speak firmly and constructively to them, is a valuable skill in handling problem people. If you tend to fume and walk away from a confrontation muttering to yourself, 'I wish I had said ...!! to that*0#!', then you need confrontation skills.

Constructively confronting people is a communication strategy which allows you to speak your mind and represent your feelings in a direct way. It is not a strategy of name calling or aggressive outbursts.

Marilyn, a product manager in a manufacturing company, was being brow-beaten daily by her boss for trivial events. She had always been a conscientious worker who enjoyed favourable relationships with her previous bosses and workmates. However, three months into her present job, she was taking sick leave and was prescribed anti-anxiety and anti-depressive medication for her work days and sleeping tablets for the nights, medications which she saw as bandaids and not cures. At work, she would characteristically store up violent feelings for several days and then explode in a fit of rage at some small, trivial event. Her relationship with her boss was the cause of these explosions, but she took her frustrations out on her friends and relatives who were abused for no apparent reason.

From early days, Marilyn had been taught that she should respect her elders and her boss, but when the boss was repeatedly disrespectful, she was left in a dilemma. Should she be nice and respectful or should she stand up for herself and confront her boss? This conflict produced emotional and physical effects which prompted a visit to a new doctor. Rather than prescribe another batch of sedatives which would only cover up the underlying problem, her doctor referred her for stress reduction and communication skills training. Here are the steps we followed.

Constructive confrontation steps

1   Learn how to relax

Learning how to relax is very important, as you want to be confident that your head is ruling your body and not vice versa. Refer to Chapter 7 for the relaxation procedure. If you are presently facing a problem person at work and do not have time to learn the relaxation technique in its entirety, then try the following. Just prior to the situation or at the first hint that your emotions are brewing, focus your mind on the word, R-E-L-A-X, and spell the letters to yourself. After you have spelled relax, take a comfortably deep breath and feel some of the tension flowing out as you exhale. These simple steps are not going to relax you completely, but they should enable you to collect your thoughts more effectively. For more thorough and long-term training, practise the relaxation technique twice daily for at least three to four months.

2 Identify the source of the problem

A critical part in managing confrontation experiences is understanding the dynamics of the problem situation. Ask yourself, What is this person doing which is causing me to get so annoyed or irritated? For example, Marilyn might find that it is her boss' apparently unfair criticisms which are the source of her upset.

3 Assess the effects upon you and your work

Having analysed the situation and located what you think is the source of the problem, try to assess what the effects are upon you and your work. In Marilyn's case, she might conclude that the constant criticism from her boss causes her work effectiveness to fall.

4 Plan your approach, your words and your behaviour

Having identified the source and the effects of the problem, plan what you will say to the problem person. Try to keep your statement short and concise. The more you ramble on, the less impact the initial statement will have. Also plan what you will do with your body language—your gestures, posture and eye contact. Standing in a stooped posture with your eyes on the ground will not advance your position. Confrontation situations require an upright stance, firm eye contact, a suitably serious facial expression, and positive use of gestures, if appropriate. Practise your lines in the bathroom in front of the mirror so that you can see and hear what you are saying. You might also want to tape record, (video or audio) your practised approach to look (listen) for areas needing some refinement.

5 Anticipate the other person's responses

Following the delivery of your statement to the problem person, it is very likely that there will be a response. Knowing the problem person, try to anticipate what sort of response to expect. You do not want to generate an argument, you just want the other person to understand the ramifications of their problem behaviour as perceived by you.

6   Choose your time and place for the approach

Try to select a time and place to meet with the problem person so that the maximum effect is derived. In the work setting, try to find a private place. Discussing your feelings and the behaviour of the other person in public could compromise your objectives and possibly alienate the other person further.

7   Following your approach, review your performance

Constructive confrontation skills are complex and intricate and will need polishing and refining. The best way to improve is to try. Having tried, then evaluate what you did—both the positive and negative aspects. It might seem risky confronting others, but in the long-term, it is far better to stand and speak rather than smother angry feelings.

8   If difficulties persist, consult a psychologist

Because confrontative communications are complex and the interchanges can be sensitive and delicate (especially if the problem person is your boss), you may benefit from discussing the problem with a psychologist. The psychologist will help you analyse the problem and prepare your approach.

In summary, becoming more constructively confronting is a most important skill when dealing with problem people. Appropriate training will help you get to the source of the problem and deal with it. You will feel better knowing how to manage problem people at work.

Putting problem solving to work

As mentioned above, problem people frequently create turmoil and dissension in the work group. Being able to stand aside from strong emotions and think logically and creatively is a most critical skill, but one which will require preparation and practice. Let's look at a series of steps which you might try to sort out a problem with a person at your workplace.

1   Treat the person with respect

Just as it often takes two people to make a problem, it frequently requires participation of the same two to reach a mutually agreeable solution. Threat and intimidation can hinder problem solving, so be certain to approach the person with composure and respect.

Jennifer was able to sort out a very sticky and difficult work problem by approaching the other party firmly and positively. Jennifer's opening words were particularly impressive: 'There seems to be a spot of bother in this matter and I'm calling to ask for your assistance in sorting out the problem.' By asking for the other person's help and assistance, there was little or no threat and a mutually agreeable solution was readily negotiated.

2   Arrange a time to discuss the problem

Many problems might be dealt with on the spot, but when considerable discussion and debate are needed, it is best to arrange another meeting so that neither party is constrained by time. There is also the factor of providing confidential conditions so that the discussion is not hampered by the presence of other interested parties.

3   Prepare for the meeting

Many people overlook the critical step of preparing for problem solving discussions because they assume they either have the answers in their head or trust that the answers will come at the appointed time. Good solutions to sticky problems can be difficult to produce and it is best not to gamble on magic or flashes of brilliance on the day.

Start a file on the problem and spend several minutes at different times of the day thinking about the problem and possible solutions. Jot down the pros and cons of each idea. Review your early thoughts and discuss them with a trusted colleague while respecting the confidence of the person with whom you will be meeting. Keep adding more thoughts to the file and don't be too worried about quality—it's quantity of ideas that you want at this stage.

Before the meeting, go through the file and try to organise your ideas into some overall plan or solution. Make some brief notes about points you want to raise during the discussion. The essence is to walk into that meeting with confidence in your preparation and yourself. Have your mind primed with some fruitful suggestions which can act as a starting point for the discussion.

4 Be positive and reinforcing during the discussion

In order to reach a favourable and workable outcome, it will be necessary to keep the discussion on a positive bearing. Be positive and reinforcing in response to good suggestions from the other person. Something like, 'Yes, that's a most interesting idea, but I would prefer to see it more like this . . .' can maintain a supportive atmosphere during your discussion.

For meetings with people who cause anger, resentment or equally strong emotions, you will need to prepare more thoroughly.

Having sorted out your thoughts and ideas, it will be helpful to spend a few minutes just prior to the meeting relaxing yourself and getting a firm control on your emotions. Once again, refer to Chapter 7 and revise the relaxation technique.

5 Follow up the decisions you reach at your meeting

As people tend to resist change, it is necessary that decisions involving substantial change be followed up in a positive fashion. Note in your diary the date at which you would like to monitor progress or reconsider the matter. Meeting with the person at that time and asking how the new approach is working out is a good practice and often results in effective people management.

Thus, working towards mutually agreeable solutions with problem people at work is a task requiring co-operation from both parties. Problem solving discussions should be characterised by respect, foreplanning and positivism. Following the meeting, the solution should be monitored to ensure that the old problem has not slowly re-emerged.

Increasing your own likeability

Harmonious and productive working relationships exist primarily because the needs of the individuals in the work team are being met. For some, there may be a need to remain quiet and removed so that they can get on with their work. For others, however, there may be a need to forge closer ties and warmer relationships with workmates. As long as the aims of the employing body are being met, then these varying needs of the work team members can be tolerated.

Problems occur, however, when this reciprocating system of need/satisfaction gets unbalanced. If one or more people want to satisfy needs which are outside the aims of the employing body or antagonistic to the other work team members, then problems occur. For example, if one person wants to manipulate the work schedule to ensure more flexitime at the expense of the others, then that person can expect some resultant turmoil in the group. As work team members often spend more time with each other than they do with their own family members, it is important to maintain positive and effective work relationships. Let's look at several ways relationships at work can be enhanced and made more harmonious and productive.

- Be pleasant.
  At the start of the work day, take a few minutes to chat briefly with your workmates nearby. A warm smile and a few friendly words can get both you and your workmates off to a positive start in the day.
- Be interested in others.
  Show an active interest in your workmates. Asking about their plans for the forthcoming weekend or showing interest in an event they mentioned casually at lunch can bring you closer to others.
- Be thoughtful.
  Remember birthdays and other special events important to your work team members. Bringing in a cake and taking time to celebrate the occasion during a coffee break can create a more friendly environment at work.
- Be generous with your time.
  Giving some time to assist workmates who need help is a good investment. The dividends are generally warmer relationships.
- Be open about yourself—but be discreet.
  Being able to talk appropriately about yourself and your life outside of work makes you a more approachable person. Of course, talking about yourself, if carried to excess, will create boredom and possibly even antagonism. Keep the conversations a two-way process.
- Be willing to spend time outside of work with others.

Your relationships with your workmates will deepen if you occasionally spend some time outside of work hours with them. A drink after work, a dinner out or a weekend activity will bring you closer to others.

- Be aware of your workmates' sensitivities.

When one of your workmates seems to be upset, offer to discuss the matter. The situation might be too personal for workplace discussion, but your offer will be appreciated. In your discussions with others in distress see the issues from their perspective and take note of their sensitivities.

- Be willing to read books on interpersonal communication and friendship formation.

If you feel estranged from others at work and would like to have closer relationships, browse through your local bookshop or library for relevant books on the topic.

- Be prepared to enroll in a communication course.

As social relationships are very complex, book reading and self-practice might not be sufficient to bring you closer to your workmates. In that case, consider joining a communication course—consult your doctor or another helping professional for suggestions about courses and other resources.

Summary

Working with a problem person can be a distressing experience. From the organisation's perspective, problem people can create dissension in the work team, increased absenteeism, decreased motivation, and decreased productivity. In any work team of ten or more people, there is a high probability that there is at least one person who creates problems for others.

This chapter has presented a mini-psychology of workplace personalities followed by several ways of dealing with problem people at work. They are:

Developing constructive confrontation skills

- Learn how to relax (See Chapter 7).
- Identify the source of the problem.
- Assess the effects upon you and your work.
- Plan your approach—your words and your behaviour.

- Anticipate the other person's response(s).
- Choose carefully the time and place for your approach.
- Following the discussion, review your performance.
- Consult a psychologist for assistance if difficulties continue with the problem person.

Problem solving

- Treat the other person with respect.
- Arrange an appropriate time to discuss the problem.
- Prepare thoroughly for the meeting.
- Be positive during the discussion.
- Follow up the decisions from the meeting.

Increasing your own likeability

- Be pleasant.
- Be interested in others.
- Be thoughtful.
- Be generous.
- Be open about yourself.
- Be willing to spend time with others.
- Be willing to read resource books.
- Be prepared to enrol in communication courses.

11

Love and hate at work

Love and hate are potent feelings which can overwhelm you, often just when your emotions can least afford the upset. For example, how often have you experienced the following situations?

- Feelings of love interfere with your concentration at work.
- You love (and sometimes hate) a person who doesn't love you.
- You hate your boss or a colleague.
- You're jealous of the attention given to a person you love.
- You love a person working nearby, but fear acting upon your feelings.
- You were in a relationship until yesterday when your partner said, Enough!

Love at your workplace can be exciting, depressing, challenging, and frustrating. Hate can be infuriating and disturbing. Love, hate and other strong emotions such as jealousy can produce havoc during your work days, not to mention your evenings and nights. While the workplace has been a well-respected place for people to meet, chat and possibly even forge long-term relationships, management generally looks disapprovingly upon love-struck workers who are spending more time pining than producing. Bosses are even less impressed with workers who are are overwhelmed with jealousy and hate. The question is, how do you experience these common emotions and deal with them constructively while also getting on with your job? This chapter will focus upon the following topics: concentrating upon your work while being in love; dealing with despair following a love affair termination; and handling jealousy and hate.

Concentrating on work when in love

Falling in, and possibly out of love can be very significant emotional experiences. The Hollywood image of the love-struck individual lost in a daze might seem overstated, but for those who have been in love, you will know the problems—excitement, exhilaration, poor concentration and questionable performance (at work, that is), to mention but a few reactions.

I recently saw a young female journalist, Chris, who was in love, but with two men. Not surprising, the strain on her emotions produced a wide array of reactions. She became chronically indecisive, occasionally depressed, at times exhilarated but often confused. She tossed and turned during her restless nights and lost her appetite. At work, she became apathetic and ineffectual.

Fortunately for Chris, her restlessness, confusion and other problems did not persist more than a few weeks. Quite un-expectedly, one of the men was offered an overseas job and he packed up and left. His sudden departure was a bitter-sweet solution to the dilemma. Chris' ego was slightly deflated that the job took precedence over her; but, on the other hand, fate had resolved her indecision. The editors were happy to see the long-awaited articles and their threats of 'produce or else' were rescinded.

Most people will not have to contend with the problem of two concurrent love affairs as did Chris. However, for those who find themselves in love and who have to still produce at work, the following suggestions may help to get you through each day.

- If your work productivity is seriously affected, consider explaining your circumstances to your boss. Being in love is a natural situation and it is generally better that your boss knows what is happening.

- Structure your time tightly so that you have specific tasks and clear cut goals throughout the day. Knowing what you want to get done in the next fifteen minutes is one way of keeping your mind from straying.

- Concentrate your love-prone thoughts into several five minute periods during the day. Do not let love thoughts infiltrate and distract you at other times.

- When phone calls are your major communication link, limit them to coffee breaks or lunch breaks. Tying the swithchboard up with yet another call to or from X can antagonise the firm.

- Keep news of your relationship under wraps except for very trusted friends. Gossip mongers can make life miserable for the love-struck individual.

- Exercise regularly to vent the accumulated emotional steam which can build up. Get out of the office at lunch time and take a brisk thirty minute walk.

- If these self-control strategies do not work, then speak with a trusted friend or professional helper.

Some of the above measures might sound Draconian, but they can help to preserve the quality of your work and possibly even your job. Love is an enjoyable emotional state, but one which needs careful control at work.

While being in love can be a major distraction and an emotional obsession, so can terminating a relationship. If your relationship is in distress and you believe it is best to end it (or you think your partner wants to end it), how can you press ahead with your work and still survive?

Dealing with an ended relationship

The end of a relationship can be accompanied by despair, despondency and even depression. You will probably know at least one person whose work performance plummeted after a relationship breakup—if you haven't experienced this misfortune yourself.

William, a product manager with a large manufacturing firm had been seeing Caroline on a steady basis for nine months when she told him one evening that there just wasn't enough in their relationship to warrant any further contact. This news came suddenly and unexpectedly and William was devastated. He did not arrive at work the next day and rang in to say he was sick and would not be at work for a week. When he did return, his colleagues remarked about how ill he still looked. William said he had a severe case of influenza and hoped to bounce back quickly. In reality, it took William months to overcome the trauma of his severed relationship. During that period, his work performance was most decidedly down. His confidence and general outlook on life were also at low ebb. Fortunately, he had the good sense to see a professional about his emotional state, a move which facilitated his recovery.

Relationship termination generally is a traumatic experience and the repercussions can last for months, possibly years. What can be done to help bounce back more quickly? Here are a few suggestions.

- Discuss the termination with your ex-partner so that you understand clearly why the relationship ended. A rational understanding can help salve the hurt feelings and help prevent avoidable mistakes from recurring.
- Consider discussing the matter with a close and trusted friend. His or her perceptions of you and your ex-partner can possibly enhance your understanding of the failed relationship.
- Try to get back into a structured routine. Strong emotional feelings are much more likely to overwhelm you when you are alone, idle and unoccupied.
- Be certain to occupy potentially lonely evenings and weekends with interesting and preoccupying activities. You can keep the blues at bay by being actively involved with friends or interesting pursuits.
- Refrain from accepting full blame for the severed relationship. Remember, it takes at least two people to create a disagreement.
- Use your newly acquired spare time (time previously spent with your partner) to take up activities which you never had time to pursue before.
- Avoid sitting at home and ruminating about the relationship. If it's over, it's over and brow beating will only give you a headache.
- Plan two or three positive events for each day. Buy yourself a special treat (avoid using food as a treat, especially if overeating can be a problem), go to a movie you've wanted to see, or ring an old friend who makes you feel good. Look forward to these events each day.
- If being in a relationship is very important to you, strike out and meet some new people. However, be cautious about rebounding from one disappointing experience into another.

Thus, a relationship termination can cause personal and occupational havoc. It is important to address the situation directly by planning your days and occupying your mind. Ruminating will only prolong the agony. If your efforts at bouncing back do not succeed, then consult a helping professional for assistance.

Hate and jealousy at work

At risk of dwelling upon the negativities of relationships, it is important to consider two very strong and most upsetting emotional states—hate and jealousy.

Most of us have experienced hate (many loving relationships have a subtle or not-so-subtle hate component). As for jealousy, you will most probably know someone, if not yourself, who is predisposed to this strong emotional state.

Let me briefly mention the case of Michael, an architectural draughtsman who is married to Lisa. Michael comes from a close-knit Southern European family and married Lisa, an attractive Australian lass, when they were both in their early twenties and when both were socially and sexually inexperienced. Even though Michael is bright, well-qualified and successful in his job, he nevertheless is pathologically jealous of his wife and any association she might have with other men. Telephone calls are monitored and friendships are scrutinised for possible amorous involvements. Lisa felt socially inhibited and constrained at parties and even at home, as Michael was always checking upon her. These checks upon Lisa created an oppressive aura of mistrust and suspicion, hardly the makings for a positive and productive relationship. Michael's tensions are carried back to his workplace where he tries to get his mind away from Lisa and onto his projects—a difficult task indeed.

Hate is an equally disturbing emotion which can pre-occupy one's mind and diminish work effectiveness. I recently counselled Kathy who worked with Veronica in the administrative section of a large national company. Kathy is quiet, conservative and conscientious in her manner and work. Veronica, as Kathy describes her, is loud, aggressive and very casual about her work. What has caused Kathy to hate Veronica is the threat that Veronica is going to win a work promotion which Kathy desperately wants. Veronica is all smiles to everyone and dashes from desk to desk chatting, gossiping and frittering away the days. Kathy, on the other hand, sits at her desk and tries to get her work done. Certainly, Janet, the supervisor of the section, is responsible for overseeing the work output and general behaviour of the workers in the section. However, Veronica seems to evade any disciplinary action by flattering Janet. When Kathy first came to see me, she feared being reprimanded because her work output was declining dramatically due to the emotional rage within her. She felt unable to compete with her articulate, yet apparently irresponsible colleague. On waking every workday, her mind immediately turned to Veronica and fire and fumes would start rising within. It is certainly difficult to work effectively and efficiently if your emotions are on the boil the entire day—and Kathy's certainly were.

Both of these short cases suggest severe problems at the workfront. Jealousy and hate make work, especially productive work, very hard going. What can be done about these difficult situations? Here are a few suggestions.

- Ask, 'Why am I reacting so strongly to that particular person or situation? How is this person posing a threat to me? Are any basic personal needs being challenged or endangered by this person?' Self understanding will help you deal with the strong feelings.

- If your self-examination is not sufficiently enlightening, ask a trusted colleague for his or her views. Sharing your feelings will help and your colleague might be able to suggest a new perspective on the problem. Just talking about the situation will often help to get the steam out of your system.

- Approaching the person who is the focus of your hate or jealousy may be threatening, but that is addressing the problem at the source. If your temper is a problem, that is, you may lose control and engage in behaviour which you would later regret, then reconsider. Cool, calculated control is necessary when dealing with a person you hate.

- If you are going to approach the provocateur, review the suggestions in Chapter Ten for dealing effectively with problem people. You will certainly want to be well-prepared. Letting your hate or jealousy loose in this meeting is not going to advance your position—in fact, you may well experience a setback.

- Try to keep your mind off the offensive person. Structure your days very carefully and fill them with tasks which will preoccupy your mind.

- Record in a notebook every time you feel the hate and/or jealousy rise to the surface. Chart the total at the end of each day. You will probably find that charting these episodes of strong feeling will help to bring them under control.

- Try to spend a small amount of time several times a day doing some exercise. Just standing and stretching can release some pent up steam and allow you to get productively back to your work.

- Do not take your aggressions out upon innocent bystanders. Family members or your poor dog or cat who greets you at home should definitely not be abused because you hate or harbour strong negative feelings about someone at work. Learn to handle your feelings and the problem people yourself.

Summary

We are emotional beings, but when strong positive or negative feelings overwhelm us, our personal and vocational lives can suffer. It is very difficult indeed to lock up and seal off our emotional reactions. However, when love, hate and jealousy become manifest in our work behaviour, it's time to act decisively to ensure that your work, and perhaps your job, do not suffer. This chapter presented some suggestions on how to handle strong emotions, including the following themes:

- Concentrating upon your work when you are in love
- Dealing with despair following the end of a love affair
- Handling jealousy and hate

12
Getting promoted, changing jobs

Are you frequently ...

- Frustrated in your job?
- Wanting more responsibility at work?
- Stale from doing the same tasks over and over?
- Looking for more challenge and excitement?
- Needing more recognition for the work you have been doing?
- Wanting more money to meet escalating personal expenses?

If you have answered Yes to one or more of the above items, then perhaps you should be seriously considering going for a promotion. The promotion might be to a more senior position in the same department or work area or, if you work in a large bureaucracy, it could be to another department.

This chapter will present several issues relevant to promotion of eligible persons. The topics to be discussed include: assessing your present job possibilities and your future opportunities; deciding whether to stay with your present job/department or look further afield; investigating new job possibilities; 'dealing' with your boss; preparing your promotion application and collecting appropriate documentation; handling the promotion interview; and making use of grievance procedures, if unsuccessful.

Assessing job possibilities

Promotion is generally a rewarding situation for the employee. To be promoted usually means that you have done a good job and the employer wants to recognise and reward you for your value to the firm. But promotion often carries with it the expectation that you will accept further responsibilities. When considering the possibility of promotion, it would benefit you to ponder the issues below:

Positive factors suggesting promotion:

- You are satisfied with the type of work you are doing.
- You are happy with the organisation for whom you are working.
- You feel comfortable and competent with your work.
- You are ready to accept more responsibility.
- You are eager for new challenges.

Reconsider applying for promotion if:

- You are not happy with your work and/or your firm.
- You lack confidence in your job skills.
- You have serious doubts about your suitability to accept more responsibility.
- You have difficulty relating well to others at your workplace.

Hopefully, you will have satisfied most if not all of the positive factors relating to promotion. However, if all is not well at the work front, you may want to consider other options to promotion at your existing job.

If you are not happy with your job, try to assess why this is and then improve the situation, if possible. If improving your situation is not possible, then consider the feasibility of leaving for another position.

If you lack confidence in your work skills, it is certainly not the time to apply for promotion. Use your time and energy instead in upgrading your skills. Enquire about in-service training programs, external job-updating courses, or evening college courses. The very fact that you are pursuing additional training will probably enhance your general confidence, hopefully upgrade your job-specific skills and perhaps even impress your boss.

Many promotions will bring extra responsibility. If this frightens you, then it's best to ask, 'Why?'. What would your increased responsibilities be and why are these potentially a problem for you? Often, increased work responsibilities involve supervising others, a delicate skill area. If you have doubts about your capabilities in handling general supervisory duties, such as reprimanding others, then ask your boss if you can take on smaller leadership responsibilities. By accepting these less threatening duties and discussing your progress with your boss, you can shape your leadership and supervisory skills.

If your relationships with one or more people at work are posing stresses and difficulties, then address the problem. Perhaps there is some misunderstanding underpinning the difficulties? Or, perhaps it's a communication problem. Browse through the Chapter 10 on working with problem people and see if any suggestions are applicable. If you can get to the base of the trouble, then you may wish to give some further thought to promotion. One thing is certain, problems between people at work can be most distressing. Unfortunately, these problems often do not go away on their own. Sit down, think through the problems, plan your course of action and then act. Dealing with problems can be risky, but solutions are not likely to come any other way.

Having decided to press ahead and think about a promotion, it is important to look down your prospective career path. If you apply for and win the promotion, are you committing yourself to a more restricted career situation? That is, does the promotion take you off the main track and on to a dead end? If so, have a careful look at other opportunities.

Other factors warranting consideration are your age, family responsibilities and financial obligations. Use the following chart to clarify where you are going with your present career and record your anticipated positions at the suggested ages.

**Your career and
Future responsibilities**

Age	Job	Appeal	Salary	Responsibilities (family, mortgage, education, etc.)
Present Age (A)				
A + 5 years				
A + 10 years				
A + 15 years				
A + 20 years				
A + X years				

Whether you are in private enterprise or a public service job, it is best to look ahead and see where your career is headed. Based upon the information recorded on the chart, do you think you will be happy with your job in, say, ten years? Will the salary cover your anticipated expenses? The chart will give you a plan to progress by, even if it is based at this stage upon educated guessing about your career prospects. Of course, careers can change in surprising directions and quite quickly. Therefore, the chart should be seen only as a guide to planning and as an aid to decision making. With reference to a decision to apply for promotion or look for a better opportunity elsewhere, pay particular attention to the job appeal notes and salary levels.

Staying or leaving

Deciding whether to stay on with your present firm or leave to work elsewhere can be a major decision. These considerations may be precipitated by unanticipated changes at work, such as a takeover of your firm. Or, you may have been experiencing a growing dissatisfaction with your work, your boss, or your colleagues. Perhaps you have been with the same organisation for several years and have met the challenges and exhausted the opportunities which the job can offer. Your days at work may have become increasingly monotonous or perhaps even downright boring. You may have been thinking quietly to yourself that maybe it's time to look elsewhere for another job.

Making this decision can be difficult—and it certainly is important. It is most important to ponder carefully the decision to leave, especially when good jobs are hard to find; when leaving means making new workplace friends; and, when you have to continue meeting your financial obligations. Under these circumstances, you just don't jump up and leave impulsively. Why not sit down and put your thoughts on to paper? You might find the following chart helpful in stimulating your thoughts about the decision.

Consider each job aspect and personal quality and record a number 1, 2 or 3 on either the stay or the leave side. The number you record represents the strength of that item for either staying or leaving. The totals at the end of the chart are a quantitative estimate to assist you in your decision making.

Deciding to stay or to leave

Stay			Job aspect	Leave		
1	2	3		1	2	3
			. . . . Job satisfaction			
			(challenge and stimulation)			
			. . . . Job commitment			
			. . . . Salary, benefits			
			potential			
			. . . . Relationship with boss			
			. . . . Relationship with co-workers			
			. . . . Career prospects			
			. . . . Family considerations			
			(move house? change kids' schools?)			
			. . . . Other job aspects			
			(list)			

Personal analysis

			. . . . Adaptability and flexibility			
			. . . . Ambition			
			. . . . Importance of job responsibility			
			. . . . Personal health			
			. . . . Job stress			
			. . . . Importance of money			
			. . . . Importance of work friendships			
			. . . . Other job-related personal qualities			
			(list)			

Totals: . . . .
To stay . . . .
To leave . . . .

Expand the chart to give a comprehensive picture of your job and you. As stated before, the chart is meant to function as a stimulus. Ensure that all relevant and important issues are given thorough consideration.

Researching new job opportunities

There are various means of finding out what is presently and potentially available on the job market, including advertised positions in the local and national papers, in-house 'Positions

Vacant' bulletins, word of mouth, visits to other organisations or departments, and registering with an employment agency.

Monitor the employment ads in your field of work. You can keep abreast of new developments and opportunities and judge how your present salary compares with other organisations. Clip the ads which look interesting and ring to get more details, even if you think you are satisfied with your present situation. If and when conditions change in your job and you want to look elsewhere, you will have a reasonably up-to-date idea of what is happening on the job market.

Many large organisations have an in-house positions vacant newsletter which is distributed throughout the company. These newsletters encourage employees with positive and established work histories to look for new opportunities in-house versus leaving the organisation. It costs time and money to advertise externally and interview and train new people, so there are considerable savings in retraining and promoting people already known to the company. Read the bulletins regularly and if a position appears which looks interesting, contact the department head or other reference person to discuss the job possibility in more detail. Once again, make notes about the position and file them in your career file for later reference.

Word-of-mouth is one of the most common means of learning about new job opportunities. Keeping one's ears and eyes alert to new developments and possible changes in the organisation can pay dividends. Departmental mergings, organisation takeovers, retirements, staff re-organisations and just normal comings and goings of other staff are all possible sources of new job opportunities. Word of these changes often filters down the corridors of the organisation. When you want to know what is going to happen in large companies, listen to what your colleagues, telephonists and receptionists have to say about new developments. No matter what the source of your information, consider the implications and possible opportunities. If the word-of-mouth information looks interesting and promising, follow it up.

Visits to other departments or organisations can be one way of pursuing possible leads. Your visit might be explicitly to meet with a departmental head to discuss job opportunities. Talk with as many people as possible at the office about new developments, policy changes and new appointments. If you like the setting and the people and if promising possibilities emerge, pursue them.

Registering with an employment agency is a relatively hassle-free way of coping with the job market. The personnel counsultant acts as a middle person between you and possible employers. The consultant's job is to find the right position for you and your skills. The consultants will know the skills required by the employer, but just as importantly, they should also be familiar with the critical people and emotional climate of the office where the vacancy exists. If you choose to deal with an employment agency, be certain to enquire about the people under whom you would work. Ask specifically about the extent of staff turnover during the previous three to five years. Generally speaking, happy work places have less staff turnover.

Brenda, a highly experienced clerical worker, was attracted to what she initially thought was a dream job. The salary was considerably higher than her existing wage and the company seemed to be very progressive. Without asking further about the company and the boss under whom she would be working, she quit her present job and moved ahead—at least that's the direction she thought she was going.

Four weeks into her new job, Brenda realised she had made a drastic mistake. The company was not as dynamic as she thought, but worse still was the situation with her boss. Her boss seemed to gloat upon demeaning her. He seemed to look for opportunities to criticise her, even when the matter was not part of her job. Brenda had enough when her boss made disparaging comments about her weight in front of other managers. She took dramatic action and slammed down the paperwork she was carrying and announced in anger that she had had enough of his insults and that she quit! One hour later, she dissolved into tears, fearing that she had made yet another mistake. Later when we met to discuss her situation, I reassured her that she acted appropriately and that her strength of character and her previous job experience would quickly win her another job.

One final job search possibility centres upon you and your ideal job. Unfortunately, many people limit their thinking and planning to the channels noted previously—the daily papers and other conventional job finding avenues. However, you know best what kind of job really appeals to you, but you may never see an ad for such a job. What can you do about this dilemma?

Several years ago, I saw a young university Arts graduate who was dismayed about the job spectrum before her. Her vision went as far as clerical work in the public and private sectors, but these jobs seemed unappealing. Her true love was music and, upon questioning, it turned out that she had been a chief organiser of several large rock concerts. I suggested she might approach the state government department which sponsored the annual public concerts. Even though there had been no advertised position, she prepared a resumé and arranged an appointment. Several months later she was employed by the department to fill a previously non-existent position! She happened to appear at the right place and right time and with the right type of experience and ideas. It's an unusual occurrence, but that's only because most people hold back from making unsolicited approaches. Get your job ideas down on paper and then list the organisations which might be interested. From that point on, knock on the doors and make yourself known. You never know what luck can bring—but keep in mind that luck favours the prepared mind.

Thus, monitoring the employment situation both inside and outside your organisation is a task which should be performed regularly. If and when you become disenchanted with your position, you have a reasonably current idea of what is available. When the time comes for a possible move, use the avenues discussed above to collect facts and meet relevant people. Having the essential information before you is the best way to progress in making the decision of to go or to stay. If you decide to stay, you may wish to do a deal with your present boss.

Dealing directly with your boss

If you have researched outside job prospects and found nothing particularly interesting, you may wish to consider how your present job situation can be enhanced by dealing with your boss. Asking for a raise in salary or other benefits presumes that you have been doing recognisably good work. If this is the case, then prepare a summary of your achievements and practise your approach beforehand. Knowing the type of person your boss is, choose a time when you are most likely to receive a positive reception.

Neil, a production manager with a large plastics firm, had been growing increasingly dissatisfied with his job. He had been complaining to his wife about his boss for the past few months and had been casting his eyes across the employment ads in the newspapers. He was interested in either getting a promotion which would place him at a comfortable distance from his present boss, or getting out of the firm to a better position elsewhere.

On a Friday afternoon at the end of a particularly disastrous week, Neil was stomping down the hall in frustration when he met his boss. In desperation, he blurted, 'Look, Jim, either we get some competent people out there on the shop floor or you can get a new production manager!'

You can guess what sort of reception Neil got late on a Friday afternoon. His boss did not want to hear about disasters at that point in the week. It would have been far preferable for Neil to go home slightly frustrated and then cool down. In a calmer state, he then could plan various options which could be used to solve the production problems. With an action plan in mind, he could approach Jim in a much more constructive way on Monday or Tuesday. Having established a more positive impression, he could then go on the discuss his own plans—to apply for promotion or discuss a move to another company. If you identify with Neil's predicament, be wary of Friday afternoon confrontations. Choose your time and place very carefully and then be well-prepared for the meeting.

When talking with your boss, emphasise your desire to continue performing well, but also mention that your interests have been drawn to the possibility of positions elsewhere. Having summarised your past accomplishments, your future interests and your potentials, you may wish to manoeuvre the conversation to what you want from your present employer. Mentioning a salary increment might bring sweat to the brow or knocks to the knees of your boss. Being well-prepared, you have anticipated how to respond to these particular behaviours. Do not demand an immediate response, but finish the discussion with the basic thought that in order to hold on to you and your skills, some additional rewards might be appropriate. It is important to reiterate that these discussions, or more appropriately put, negotiations, are sensitive and delicate matters and will require careful preparation, appropriate anticipation and thorough practice.

Applying for promotion

In large organisations and government bureaucracies, applications for promotion generally have to be submitted to the central administration, usually the personnel division. As their decision will, to a large extent, depend upon the advice they receive from your immediate boss, discuss your plans with your boss before lodging your official application.

Your boss may advise you that there are periodic promotion reviews of staff and applications are to be lodged only during these review periods. Additionally, there might be a set form to fill in. Whether there is a set form or not, you will undoubtedly want to summarise your work history with the organisation, and emphasise your special responsibilities, skills and noteworthy accomplishments. Backup references will probably not be required, but you may wish to append substantiating documentation (letters, reports, etc.) to amplify your major points. The application should be thorough, but not too lengthy.

Handling the promotion interview

In large organisations and government bureacracies, there might be several people applying for the same promotion position. One way of processing the applicants is to call them for an interview. There are several points you will want to consider before attending a promotion interview.

1 Plan your approach

Try to establish who will be on the interviewing panel. Take into account the personalities of these people when thinking through your interview approach.

2 Prepare your materials

Write out on a note card the major issues which you wish to discuss during the interview. You can count on one question being asked of you at the end of the interview: Do you have any questions which you would like to ask?

Consult your note card or your memory at this point and raise any outstanding issues.

If your job is one where drawings, documents or other materials might be of interest and help, have them with you and think ahead how you might use these resources. Do you need a stand, projector or other equipment? If so, be certain that suitable provision is made beforehand.

3 Peform as calmly as possible

If calmness under interview conditions is not your strong suit, then learn how to relax by reading Chapter 7.

During the interview, do not feel you have to blurt out an instantaneous answer to each question. There is considerable advantage in pausing for a few seconds, pondering the issue and then responding. Silence can be a powerful tool for the calm, composed and confident interviewee.

4 Ponder your strengths and weaknesses following the interview

Acquiring effective interviewing skills is a matter of experience. Rather than breathe a sigh of relief and forget the whole gruelling experience, go back to your work place and make some notes about your strong and weak points during the interview. Review these notes prior to succeeding interviews.

Appeal or grievance procedures

Once again, for those who work in large organisations, there may be established procedures to use if you think you have been unfairly passed over in a promotion judgment. It is important to note that once a bureaucratic decision has been made, especially a decision reached by several individuals on an interviewing panel, it is unlikely that the decision will be reversed unless new and substantive information is being presented. In addition to matters of fact, there can, however, be appeals based upon procedural issues, such as discriminatory treatment and bias. These are very sensitive matters and before lodging an appeal based upon these grounds, it is advisable to obtain legal advice from a very experienced personnel consultant. A person outside of your organisation may be able to offer an independent judgment, but also consult relevant people in the system. If you think you have a case to be heard, do not be intimidated by the formalities of the procedures. Seek support for your case from experienced helpers at government grievance authorities or from private counsel.

Summary

Promotion possibilities are very important to the person who is a committed and keen worker. Promotion, when it is achieved, can function as a stimulus, a new challenge and a personal reward for work well done. However, when promotion is not feasible or a likely possibility, then a job change might be considered. This chapter has presented the following issues about promotion and job change:

- Assessing your present job possibilities and future opportunities
- Deciding whether to stay or to leave your job
- Charting your future career
- Researching for new job opportunities
- Dealing with your present boss
- Applying to the administration for promotion
- Handling the promotion interview
- Using appeal or grievance procedures if your promotion application is unsuccessful

13

Changing career, getting dismissed, retiring

Do you often ...

- Question whether you should pursue a new career?
- Back away too quickly from new occupational possibilities because of family obligations and responsibilities?
- Dream about being in your own business?
- Hold back from updating your resume?
- Fear getting dismissed from your job?
- Think that retirement will be the ideal solution to all or most of your work worries?

People who are unhappy at work can dwell upon the types of issues listed above. This chapter will address some practical approaches whereby you can deal with job distress, instead of worrying about it. The issues to be discussed include: preparing for a possible career change; drafting your resume; considering starting your own business; coping with dismissal; and planning for retirement.

Preparing for a career change

Having analysed your present employment situation using the stay or leave chart in the preceding chapter, you may have come to the decision that it's time to consider a new career. This goes well beyond just getting another job doing the same type of work. Starting a new career is like leaving a very familiar park pathway and taking a trembling step into a foreboding forest full of possible dangers.

If changing your career seems attractive and alluring, then it's very important to get some outside views on the matter. Discuss your thoughts about a career change with your spouse or partner and perhaps a trusted work colleague. Getting objective opinions from people who know you well is very important as employment decisions can be emotional concerns. You want your future work to be determined by firm rational decision making and certainly not by emotional and impulsive action.

If your own thoughts and your friends' advice suggest that a move is warranted, then the next question is, What careers should I consider? Hopefully, you will have various possibilities in mind and you will have been keeping abreast of new developments and opportunities in these fields of interest. While perusals of newspaper ads, employment bulletins and other information sources may have been cursory and casual in the past, the situation now requires a much more specific approach.

Career exploration is best done in a methodical way. Start a file on new career possibilities. Write the names of your career choices at the top of separate pieces of loose leaf notebook paper. Think widely and don't be too cautious at this stage. The initial goal is to get down as many ideas as possible.

Having started your file, jot down the following subcategories under each career title.

Career title
    Salary
    Qualifications required
    Personal qualities desirable
    Technical skills necessary
    Additional training needed
    Employment location
    Career prospects
    Long-term financial prospects

Leave space under each heading for jotting down information as it is collected. If you use a computer, the information can be recorded using a filing program such as the Personal File System or Cardbox. Spend some time each day working on information collection. Your thoughts will become more focused and clear as the details are obtained and filed.

Periodically, sift through your career categories and filter out those which appear to be impractical or unrealistic based upon the information you have at hand. Just as employers form a short list of applicants for a job, your task is to form a similar short list of careers which you want to pursue further.

Having formed a short list, discuss the list with your spouse, partner or close friend. Additionally, you may also wish to obtain the advice of a financial advisor, such as an accountant, bank manager or some other similar resource person. Detailed financial advice will be particularly important if you presently have considerable family responsibilities or a complicated employee benefits package. Just sorting out the pros and cons about superannuation can be a difficult matter for the financially inexperienced person. Be sure to send along the relevant financial documents prior to your interview so that the financial advisor has time to study them thoroughly before your appointment.

With your thoughts focused upon a short list and with the benefit of detailed information from various expert advisors, it may be very helpful to make a few prospecting visits to organisations which have the type of jobs which interest you. Don't be put off by the fact that there have not been any employment ads for the positions of interest. Your purpose at this stage is to get a gut feeling for the people doing that type of job and for the places where these careers are common. If your general reactions are positive, take the next step—approach the employing person or the personnel office to make your interest known.

The ideas suggested above are essentially self-initiated tasks. You may also go to various resource people, such as a psychologist specialising in career counselling, for assistance in finding the most appropriate employment area for you. The important point to keep in mind is that you want to explore yourself and your interests so that you can find as much satisfaction as possible in your next job.

Exploring new careers

Having thought through the career possibilities and assessed the advice given by the resource people you consulted, it is time to consider the market—what jobs are available to you? Depending upon the type of work you do, or would prefer to do, there may be a specialised employment service available to help. For example, in most cities there will be agencies specialising in secretarial and receptionist services, computer personnel, and technical sales people, to name but a few. For managerial positions, management consultants can be approached. Generally, the fees for placing an applicant are paid by the employer, but there might be some service fees payable by the applicant.

If you have a very convincing personality and some ideas which may be attractive to a particular industry, you might want to try advertising your services. It might sound egocentric, but it has worked for some. I know of a young man, Alan, who wanted to break into the TV/film industry. He spent two hundred dollars to place an ad in a national weekly newspaper which is widely read by people in film work. The ad said something like: Ambitious and talented young man wanting to contribute enthusiasm and ideas to a film production unit. Potential limited only by opportunity. Contact . . .' The ad appeared on a Thursday and he was invited for an interview that Saturday. On Monday he was hard at work with the television station which responded to his ad. While such an approach might sound brazen, it worked—but I should say that Alan had the confidence and talent to back up his ad.

Preparing your resumé

There are many excellent references on resume preparation, some of which are obtainable from government employment services. I will not go into detail here, other than to mention a few guidelines.

- Be brief. Try to keep your resume to one or two pages.
- Ask yourself what information an employer would want to have about you, given the type of positions for which you will be applying.
- Use the following headings to facilitate reading:
  Name
  Address
  Telephone
  Personal details
  Work experience
  Qualifications
  Other details
  References
- Structure your work experience section by listing your positions proceeding from the present backwards if you have had only a few jobs. If you have had many jobs and are concerned about being labelled a 'job hopper', then compose your work experience section by job skills.

- If you have had little relevant job experience, then consider your outside activities to see if you can list some leadership experiences or other relevant skills.
- Make a draft version of your resume and take it to an experienced person for comment.
- Experiment with various types of page layout to achieve maximum presentability and readability.
- Have your resume typed.
- Read through the resume to be certain there are no errors in spelling, grammar or syntax.

Having prepared a resume, you will want to custom adapt it to the different jobs for which you are applying. A computer is especially helpful in editing the basic form. If you have access to a computer, put your resume on file so that it can be updated and changed with minimal trouble.

Starting your own business

Most people who have become disenchanted with their job consider the possibility of starting their own business. There are certain definite appeals to being your own boss—no-one to look over your shoulder, time at work determined by you, and financial rewards contingent upon your work input.

While the picture may look very rosy and alluring, there are certain pitfalls as well. You are solely responsible for the progress of the business and that will often mean longer hours and higher pressure. If the business involves employing others, there will be stresses and strains in managing your staff. Instead of being the applicant with hat in hand, you will be the boss making the hiring and firing decisions, a position of considerable responsibility and stress.

There are certain personal qualities which have been found to be characteristic of successful entrepreneurs. Ask yourself if you feel comfortable with the following profile:

Are you ...

- Confident in your own abilities?
- Technically skilled in the specific business area of interest?
- Strongly determined to succeed?

- Highly organised and a dependable achiever?
- Vigorous?
- In very sound health?
- Skilled in handling people?
- Ambitious?

If you have answered enthusiastically, Yes!! to each of the above items, then you might be just the person to forge ahead and ultimately succeed in your own business. Before you tender your resignation to your present boss, however, it is prudent to observe the basic fact that many small businesses fail each year, often because the self-employed person has not done sufficient planning and/or because the individual has been falsely optimistic about personal skills and abilities.

Before you go any further along the road to self-employment, there are several preparatory steps which you might want to take:

1 Speak with other people in the same business field. Listen to their experiences and learn from them. Ask what contributes to the successes and failures in that type of business.
2 Consult a good accountant and your bank manager.
3 Read relevant trade publications.
4 Seek advice from the state government's small business advisory service.

A friend who had been working as a management consultant in a large accounting firm finally resigned to start his own consultancy business. This move was made, however, only after very thorough research had been carried out. Dennis consulted with various resource people and had prepared a very conservative five-year financial plan based upon projected income and expenses. A very important person in the planning stages was Dennis' wife, Shirley, who insisted that ample consideration be given to educational expenses and holiday provisions for the family. The systematic forward planning and the determination and dedication to make the business venture work have proved to be most worthwhile. There is simply no substitute for careful thinking and conscientious application when thoughts turn to self-employment.

Coping with dismissal

One of the most traumatic experiences for any worker is to get dismissed. No matter how gently the news might be given, losing one's job is still a major loss experience. If your work has not been satisfactory and you have had at least one warning meeting with your boss, then the dismissal message might not be a surprise. However, the news is seldom cheerfully received.

The immediate emotional response to being dismissed might be any of the following: anger; numbness; denial; or perhaps even apathy. Whatever your response, you will want to summon your practical senses. If for no other reason, it can be a beneficial learning experience to understand exactly why your work was not considered to be satisfactory. Ask for specific details. Was it the quality of my work? Or was it the quantity of work produced? Was it a personality aspect which caused the problem? These can be difficult questions to ask, but it is very important to know the answers.

While discussing details with your ex-boss, you can actually be in an advantageous bargaining position. There are two issues you might wish to raise. One, bargain strongly for as much severance pay as you can get. Your boss is probably feeling just as uncomfortable as you, so you can be in a strong bargaining position. In higher management circles, you may be able to argue for job relocation expenses—the employer pays fees to a management consultant to assist you in finding another position. The second matter which should be raised is a letter of reference. Be certain to discuss the terms with which your dismissal will be described.

After you have recovered from the shock of being dismissed from your job, what do you do? As you might be feeling depressed and despondent, it is important to get started on building some new possibilities for yourself. After all, getting dismissed from a job can be viewed as a positive opportunity to pursue a new career. Here are some suggestions to make those difficult days a bit more positive and productive.

- Definitely work to a daily plan and keep your days structured.
- Get out and get going early each day so that you don't sit at home feeling sorry for yourself.

- Tell a friend what you will be doing each day and report your progress. Knowing that someone else is very interested in how you are faring can make you press ahead more diligently.

- Try to get some vigorous exercise at least three to five times per week to blow off pent up emotional steam.

- Contact old friends and acquaintances who might have useful leads about new job possibilities.

- Resist the temptation to hide yourself or your situation from friends and relatives. Even the most successful people have had some employment setbacks.

- List your positive features and qualities on paper so that you don't lose sight of your strengths.

Planning for retirement

Retirement is a joy to some and a misery to others. The reaction for the latter group can be so extreme that retirement can almost be seen as a death sentence. Without getting too moribund, let me say that retirement is a concern which all too often is put on the shelf until the retirement period arrives. If not sufficient forethought has been given to this important period of one's life, the retired individual can sit perplexed and despondent, wondering how to occupy each day.

The ideal preparation for retirement is performed during the working years when the vigour is there to establish hobbies and interests and make productive plans.

James was a career public servant who had been head of his department for the eight years preceding his retirement. At his retirement party, many of his co-workers asked about his plans. He replied that he would probably just potter around the house and garden. Potter he did. As he wasn't really a fix-it type person and he disliked dirty finger nails and other gardening by-products, he roamed the house and garden much like a frustrated caged animal. James' wife was the person who sought counselling, as she was finding it more and more difficult to tolerate his growing irritability and restlessness.

The precipitating event which brought the problem to a head

was James' decision to re-organise the kitchen cabinets. He told his wife that workplace efficiency was paramount and that her kitchen was hopelessly disorganised. The kitchen battle over the placement of pots and pans almost brought a marriage of thirty-eight years to an end. Fortunately, they had the good sense to seek counselling. After several sessions, James realised that he had to develop his own interests and leave the kitchen to his wife. He found it difficult to forge into new areas, but he now has several weekly commitments, including reading for blind people, learning to play golf and serving on several committees where his previous expertise can be fruitfully used.

As in James' case, working too hard during the employment years so that one can relax in retirement is very short-term thinking. For one thing, time is necessary to learn skills and develop interests which can be nurtured through the maturing years. The other problem is that working too hard during the early and middle employment years might precipitate an early termination. It is not uncommon to hear about people who have worked themselves to death.

Some organisations are recognising the value of encouraging their employees to develop recreational interests. In addition to helping the employee deal with future retirement, the recreational interests add diversity to the working week. If your organisation has employee recreational programs, consider taking part in them to develop your interests.

One retirement activity which is worth mentioning to untiring entrepreneurs is starting yet another business. In the latter years, the entrepreneur may not want to do battle with the strong market forces, but may still derive satisfaction from doing one's own thing. Let me mention an example. A retired vicar whom I know felt the strong need to keep actively involved. I guess being a vicar can be seen in some ways as an entrepreneurial activity. At retirement, the vicar took up wood turning as a hobby and derived much personal satisfaction from his work at the lathe. The products of his hobby were so appealing that friends started commissioning work from him. As word spread, more and more requests came in, such that the vicar invested in a larger lathe. Today, the vicar runs a thriving small business keeping him interested and satisfied during his retirement period.

Retirement, therefore, is a period to be planned for and then pursued with interest and enthusiasm. Think ahead during your working years so that you have the personal skills and resources for this important period of your life.

Summary

This chapter has presented issues which arise at the end of an employment period. Termination of employment might have come about through voluntary changing of career and job, through dismissal, or by retirement. It is important to plan and prepare for these changes so that maximum advantage and learning can be achieved. The following topics were discussed in this chapter:

- Preparing for a possible career change
- Considering starting your own business
- Coping with dismissal
- Planning for retirement

References

Benson, H. *The Relaxation Response* New York: Avon Books, 1975

Berne, E. *What Do You Say After You Say Hello?* New York, NY: Bantam Books, 1973

Bolles, R. *What Color Is Your Parachute? A Practical Manual for Job-Hunters and Career-Changers* Berkeley, CA: Ten Speed Press, 1980

Buscaglia, L. *Personhood: The Art of Being Fully Human* Thorofare, NJ: C.B. Slack, 1978

DeBono, E. *Lateral Thinking* New York, NY: Harper & Row, 1973

Ellis, A. and Harper, R. *A New Guide to Rational Living* No. Hollywood, CA: Wilshire Book Co., 1977

Feldenkrais, M. *Awareness Through Movement* New York, NY: Harper & Row, 1972

Fensterheim, H. and Bear, J. *Don't Say Yes When You Want To Say No* New York, NY: Dell, 1975

Fletcher, C. *The New Complete Walker* New York, NY: Alfred A. Knopf, 1978

Forgas, J. *Interpersonal Behaviour: The Psychology of Social Interaction* Sydney: Pergamon Press, 1985

Greenberg, H. *Coping with Job Stress* Englewoodcliffs, NJ: Prentice-Hall, 1980

James, M. and Jongeward, D. *Born to Win* New York, NY: Signet Books, 1978

Johnson, D. *Reaching Out* Englewood Cliffs, NJ: Prentice-Hall, 1972

Konn, R. *Mega-Nutrition* New York, NY: McGraw-Hill Book Co., 1980

Kübler-Ross, E. *On Death and Dying* New York, NY: Dell Publishing Co., 1978

Lakein, A. *How to Get Control of Your Time And Your Life* New York, NY: Peter A. Wyden, Inc., 1973

LaRouche, J. and Ryan, R. *Strategies for Women at Work* New York, NY: Avon Books, 1984

Morris, D. *Man Watching* London: Cape Publishing Co., 1977

Peale, N. *Power of Positive Thinking* New York, NY: Fawcett, 1978

Ryan, R. and Travis, J. *Wellness Workbook* Berkeley, CA: Ten Speed Press, 1981

Samuels, M. and Benett, H. *The Well Body Book* New York, NY:

Random House, 1973

Simon, S., Howe, L. and Kirschenbaum, H. *Values Clarification* New York, NY: Hart Publishing Co., 1972

Terkel, S. *Working* New York, NY: Pantheon/Random House, 1974

Zilbergeld, B. *Male Sexuality* New York, NY: Bantam Books, 1980

Index